THE AMERICAN ENTREPRENEUR

VOLUME II

NAVIGATING THE UNEXPECTED

Business Wizards Share Their Strategies
for Thriving in a Post-COVID World

KATHLEEN TRACY

The American Entrepreneur Volume II
NAVIGATING THE UNEXPECTED

Copyright 2020 Creative Classics Publications Inc.

Graphics and layout: jcruise797@gmail.com

ISBN: 978-1-7352724-2-9

Printed in the United States of America

Table of Contents

Introduction

Even in the best of times, the road to business success requires finding ways for a brand to stand out from the competition, establishing efficient operations, optimally aligning systems, and developing strategies to increase consumer engagement and loyalty. While some companies have the resources to advance each of these areas internally, most don't—especially start-ups and emerging businesses where owners or managers wear many hats.

But these are not the best of times. Between the global pandemic, daily routines upended, and a challenging economy, businesses need to optimize their brands' potential and identify unique opportunities more than ever. The companies and business leaders profiled in this book share the strategies, vision, and wisdom gained from lessons learned in creating successful, sustainable enterprises that will not just help your business survive but thrive in a post-COVID-19 world.

ACE Consulting - Division One

Every year the US government offers small businesses the opportunity to bid on billions of dollars worth of state and federal jobs, covering everything from logistics to publishing brochures. But one particularly thriving area of opportunity is construction.

Unlike industries where you build a client base by calling or meeting potential customers in person to pitch your value proposition, seeking government work is a different animal. Most contracts are secured through open—as opposed to blind—bids. The prospective employer lists a set of requirements and specifications every bidder has to meet. To win the contract you have to meet those requirements and offer the best price and value.

The upside of contracted government work is its stability; the downside is navigating the multifaceted procedure to get your foot in the Fed's door. There's a registration process, knowing the terms of each type of contract, a bidding process that includes a proposal, and marketing your business so target agencies can see its value and fit. To succeed it's crucial the bidder understands the contractor's requirements and evaluation criteria to achieve full compliance.

For those new to bidding on government contracts, the process can seem very daunting. Some companies slog through many months or even years struggling through a long trial and error learning curve before earning and successfully completing their first contract. Other companies call ACE Consulting.

Founded by Navy Seabee veteran Scott Arias, Kentucky-based ACE has special expertise helping clients with the Department of State, Naval Facilities Command, and the Army Corps of Engineers contracts. "Our primary focus is on federal and state construction," Scott says. "And we focus on Division One services that include schedules, safety officers, quality control managers, site superintendents, pre-construction services, project administration, and on-site supervision for the construction."

ACE serves clients all over the globe, from small 8A to disabled-veteran-owned companies. "We also provide services to billion-dollar corporations, so our clientele is very diverse. We provide planning services before construction that are required by our client's customers. We help navigate the bureaucracy both off-site and on-site with our management staff. After the pre-construction requirements are completed, we provide on-site personnel to manage the actual construction through execution."

Scott's management experience is expansive, covering operations, facility, sales, quality control and assurance, and safety management. He has a veritable alphabet soup of degrees, specialties, and certifications: PhD in construction; project management professional; planning and scheduling professional; certified professional constructor; safety trained supervisor construction; environmental compliance supervisor; and is a Seabee combat warfare specialist. Impressive in any context. Much more so for a high school drop out.

Born and raised in New Mexico, Scott says he grew up in a small town forty miles outside of Albuquerque. "People always say: *Oh, I love Santa Fe*. Well, most of New Mexico is not Santa Fe," he laughs. "Poverty is pretty common, and I grew up in an impoverished culture. My parents were janitors who worked hard, but I knew I wanted something else."

Scott's brother was in the Navy. And every six months when he

Scott Arias

visited, he was driving a new car. The military offered both opportunity and stability.

"So I dropped out of high school to join the Navy. I looked at my options and felt the military was very viable. I might have joined the Navy out of necessity, but in hindsight going down that road was the best decision I ever made. But it was a difficult ride, for sure."

Since Scott had worked a lot in construction growing up, he naturally gravitated toward that in the Navy Seabees. "It's something I really enjoy. I like the satisfaction of seeing something built."

Eight years in, his military career took an unexpected turn when Scott lost his lower left leg in a motorcycle accident. After a long and difficult rehab, he returned to active duty for three more years and was deployed to the Middle East. During much of that time, Scott was continuing the educated he had interrupted when joining the Navy as a teen.

"I got my GED but didn't start college until I was twenty-five and then pretty much spent the next fifteen years going to school. I earned two associate degrees, then a bachelor's, and just kept going until I had a PhD."

While in the service, that meant studying in between his other duties. "Days, nights, weekends—when I was in Iraq. I was doing income tax accounting, sitting on top of a Conex box in the Persian Gulf," he says. "And this was when you snail-mailed all your homework in. The worst grade I ever got in a class was a C, but in my defense I earned that C because I did it in the middle of Persian Gulf on an oil platform." Possibly the best homework excuse ever.

But then while in the Middle East, he reinjured his leg and had to be medevacked out. So after twelve years of military service, Scott retired and for a while worked at building United States embassies overseas.

"I had a dream of being a CEO of a major corporation," he says. "And then one day I had an epiphany. I went to a meeting at a billion-dollar company. Three of my four bosses were there. After that meeting I realized I didn't want to be like those guys. I also realized that everybody else was getting the benefits of all the difficult work I went through getting the job done. I thought: *You know what? I can make more money with a lot less stress.* I needed to do my own thing. That's when I pulled the trigger and took the leap to start my own company."

Considering his background, starting a construction business seemed like a natural fit. "And there was a market for disabled veteran contractors," he adds. "So I did VA work for about two years until the market dried up in 2008 because of the recession."

With banks not lending money, the housing industry in the toilet, and the economy imploding, contractors around the country started looking for a source of work. "Everybody went from private work into government work because that was the only place with money."

At that point Scott changed his business model. "I decided if you can't beat them, join them. I knew how to do federal work, so I thought: *Why not help contractors who do that?* So I began consulting."

Or more precisely, tried to start consulting. It began as a part-time, one-man effort, and months went by with no business.

"At times I felt like giving up, but I kept at it and finally got my first contract after nine months. That first year we did $7,000 in revenue. In 2019 we grossed $10 million in revenue and have almost eighty staff."

ACE—named for his four children Allison, Christian, Cole, and Erin—helps contractors through the pre-construction phase, providing plans, and all the administrative paperwork. "There's a lot of red tape in the government, fortunately or unfortunately, but a lot is necessary, like construction schedules, safety plans, and quality control plans. We also provide training and field staff once the job starts. We do everything to get the project started."

Over time the consulting side of the business overtook the construction side to where now ACE does limited physical construction. The reason for the rebranding was rooted in Scott's unique skill sets.

"I thought: *What do I have that other people in my industry don't have?* Anybody could get some money together and try to execute construction. But what made me different was I understood the thinking end of it. Because I was already in the federal government doing construction, I understood how to do all those administrative and management items. That's my strength. It was something that fit within my skill set, so it was kind of a natural transition. It was a niche market, and when I looked around there was nobody doing that work. And there still isn't. We're the only solution-based company out there in construction administration and management. My specialty was the administrative side, and most contractors were doing that internally at the time."

Despite the new business direction, Scott retains the love of hands-on building and misses it. "A lot of people that I'm associated with never get their hands dirty. But I started out as a carpenter and a mason, and I still enjoy actually getting my hands dirty and do that in my free time now, pretty much every day. It's my hobby. But I visit jobs often, and it's pretty interesting. It's exciting being part of construction, going out there every day to see what's going on."

While the bulk of ACE's work is with clients doing government work, Scott says about 20 percent of the business is with private clients. "There's a lot more private work than there is public," he explains. "So we have entered the private market, and the requirements for the government are much more stringent than they are in the private industry. They still need construction schedules on private projects, but they're far less complex administratively than they are on a government job."

For as frustrating as all the red tape in government can be, its intent is to maintain a standard. "If you look comparatively at the government's records on the way they deal with quality, safety, and productivity, the government is far better in those aspects. And I think it's fair to say that federal jobs do a lot more in making sure people are safe than a private project. There are some environmental things that are over the top, but at the end of the day, I personally think everybody should be making sure we leave the environment the way we found it. They have less rework and fewer issues in construction because of their processes. Is it more costly and time-consuming? Yes, at times. But I would much prefer to have a contractor who worked on a federal job work on my home than having someone in residential because the standards of the people is much higher."

As the consulting company has grown, and the number of employees increased, Scott's role evolved. He's gone from a fledgling consultant doing everything to a CEO guiding both the company's strategic vision and implementing the culture and mission statement. Many of the people who now work for ACE are Scott's former students and faculty. During the time he was establishing the consulting company, he taught at Eastern Kentucky University, becoming a tenured professor.

"I taught construction management for twelve years," he says. "During that time I ran across a lot of good people. So I kept in touch with and made relationships with those people, and they eventually came to work with me. A lot of people I mentored through school now work with me every day. I found good people and didn't use age as a determining factor for performance. I just figured out what their skill set was and then put them in those positions and basically taught them what I learned. That freed me to focus on what I should be doing for a company of eighty people rather than the daily day in, day out tasks."

Scott taught at Eastern Kentucky until 2018 when the demands of ACE grew too big. "I'm a big believer that you're either all in or all out. It got to a point where the company was so big, I could no longer do it with all my energy and all my power, that I couldn't just go through the motions, so it was time to move on. I'm still passionate about it, though, and teach one to two classes there each year."

Scott says settling into the role of CEO was fairly easy, in part because of lessons learned in the military. "I was a chief petty officer in the Navy, and one of the things that teaches you is delegation is key to growth. To elevate, you have to delegate."

Of course knowing you need to give up some duties is one thing, doing it is another. "The hardest thing for me was giving up being *the* technical expert," Scott says. "Now I have guys who far exceed my technical expertise. Their skillset is way above mine, and that's tough to admit because that was my forte. I taught it for ten years and did it for twenty years. But I also realized my greatest skillset is the ability to develop relationships. I do enjoy talking to people; I enjoy helping people, and that's what I get to do every day now."

Not only does he help people professional by providing professional consulting, through ACE Scott also helps others and his community. Front and center on its website is ACE's Christian-based mission statement.

"We are different than most companies because we give 15 percent of every dollar we earn to a charity in support of helping our fellow man and building God's kingdom here on Earth. We are people who believe that our local church should be the solution to our problems."

Many entrepreneurs are devout or live faith-based lives, but it's not often reflected in the mission statement so transparently. But it was important to Scott that he acknowledge the importance faith plays in his life and work.

"When I lost my leg, I had a really tough time physically, mentally," he says. "I was in a dark place. The accident happened two days after I was promoted to chief petty officer, and it felt like everything I had worked for in the Navy and life was gone. It was so unfair. Going through prescription drug addiction, I finally got to the point where I wanted to commit suicide. I didn't want to live my life anymore."

It became very apparent to Scott that the only way he was going to make it through his grief and despair was through someone bigger than himself. "I went to see my chaplain. We talked for two hours, but all I remember him saying was: *We don't know what God's will is for our life. All we can do is pray to accept his will.*"

He went home and picked up an issue of *Guidepost*, which he describes as a *Reader's Digest* for Christians. "My mother-in-law had sent them to me for years, and I was reading a story about a lady who had lost her daughter. And the last line of the story was: *We don't know what God's will for our life is; all we can do is pray for our acceptance of his will.* I felt like God was personally telling me something. *Hey, listen; I have a plan for you. Just trust me. Go do the best you can, and I'll take care of the rest.* From that, I felt like I could go on."

Scott says people are often surprised at his faith. "They say: *I wouldn't get you're a Bible thumper.* I mean, I have numerous tattoos," he jokes. "I'm a construction worker and a sailor, so I often use colorful language. I'm not the stereotypical Christian by any stretch of the imagination. Once into it I realized there's a stereotypical way a Christian is supposed to be. I think the reason a lot of people don't believe isn't because God has done us anything wrong but because we as his followers have been a very poor example. Most people are reluctant to say they're

Christian, afraid to say: *Hey, this is what I believe in.* So I try to live my life and walk that line."

Scott says the non-denominational church he attends is inclusive, not judgmental. "I tell people all the time that I'm the most flawed person you'll ever come across. Who am I to judge anybody? People at my church understand we are all sinners. None of us are greater than the other because we all sin, and that's the truth. Jesus Christ came here with a message of grace, and that's what we should do for everyone. We should provide others grace because we also need grace."

When ACE first started getting traction and growing, there was no official mission or vision statement, even though those beliefs guided Scott as a person and as an entrepreneur. He says trying to always do the right thing is in his heart—something that can be a challenge in his industry.

"The construction industry is extremely unethical," Scott says bluntly. "There are a lot of people who will do anything to make a dollar. But I made a conscious choice that I didn't want to be that way. I want to be something different. I also felt a strong calling to give a percentage of what the company earns to the church or to charity."

Scott's concern was coming across as either calculated or perhaps even disingenuous. "I don't want to come across as: *Hey, look at me. See what I'm doing*—basically using God as a marketing tool. That's not what I'm doing. The only reason I put it on my website is because I feel there are not enough people saying: *I'm trying to follow the way, and I hope you will too.* And I've gotten some negative feedback, had people tell me that I'm using faith for my benefit. That never occurred to me, I saw it from the opposite side of the coin. So there have actually has been more drawbacks than benefits to living out my faith."

Another issue is that some clients expressed discomfort having their money be donated to a Christian charity. Scott says he gets it.

"Not everybody in my company is a Christian, and you have to respect the fact that in a company not everybody believes the same thing. I have some very close friends in my company who are not believers. But they respect my belief and they respect why I believe it. They're on board that I'm willing to sacrifice for the greater good, and they wrap their arms around it."

To make the mission statement more encompassing, now instead of donating money to Scott's church, ACE donates the 15 percent to a Christian foundation that helps the company allocate money and funds to different charities that employees get to choose. He estimates that in 2020, ACE donated $200,000.

"That's just not my money, that's everybody's money. We use it to buy a single mother a car, to help out a veteran—things that are near and dear to my people's heart. I have never been in this for the money, nor will I ever be. Money is nice to have, it can buy you some nice things, and I like cars and guns and watches. But in the end money is not why I run this company. We're not in business just to do construction planning and administration; we're in business because we want to make a difference. We are in the business of building the kingdom. I do this because I really want to change people's lives, and I have a chance to do that using this platform."

Scott has found that within his company, tying the work to something bigger has been good for morale and the culture. "It has inspired people to work harder, to be committed to do things that most employees would not do. Actually, we don't really have employees. We have associates. And I have already started laying the groundwork to turn ACE into an employee-owned company so everybody will own a piece."

Part of giving back to the community is sharing the lessons he's learned with others looking to start their own entrepreneurial journey. And

Scott says his lesson number one is that cash is king.

"Cash is always an issue. To get where we are today, I've leveraged everything I have and had to borrow money from high interest loan providers. My wife and I made a lot of personal sacrifices, living at a lower level to build the business. That was our conscious decision, and now it's paying off. It obviously sucks when you're doing it. But that's part of being an entrepreneur. I'm not in this to do it mediocre; I'm in this to do something significant."

Second on his list is that business metrics are imperative to success. "I'm an analytical person, and the metrics-based structure provided to me by the military translated well into business," he says. "One thing I see consulting is that most companies do not have or use metrics, and this is why they fail. You need to know total overhead or your percent of overhead. How can you make decisions if you don't have all the information in front of you? Especially for a veteran, take your military mission-oriented mindset and make your goals clear for your team, then execute. Clarity and focus are key to getting the desired outcome in business."

A corollary to that is maintaining personal discipline and consistency. Scott compares it to working out. If you only work out a day here or there, you won't be successful. But if you work out every day, even if for just twenty minutes, after six months there will be significant change.

"That consistent, deliberate discipline action is key. And that's one thing the Navy taught me. When I first joined, I had a bit of a quitter mentality, and the service broke me of that. I really didn't have a choice," he jokes. "You can't quit the service, so you either get with it or get booted. So I learned there is no such thing as quitting. I learned to show up on time and work hard. I learned to have a good attitude. Those are things you can master regardless of your innate intelligence or skill capabilities. And they go a long way to achieving success."

Scott says perhaps the biggest difference between entrepreneurs and others is their tolerance for risk. Nowhere is no risk, no reward truer than with start-ups. Scott jokes that his risk tolerance has been off the charts at times, which has earned him the nickname Loose Cannon.

"You have to be willing to lay everything you have on the line to develop a company. If you're not willing to take the risk, do not go down this road. Because at different times during the whole process, you're going to fail—multiple times. You're going to make mistakes; you're going to lose. But you have to be persistent and willing to roll the dice. The hard thing for me is that I'm now in less of a position to roll the dice, but I still want to," he laughs. "And sometimes I still do. And it can scare the living hell out of people."

Hence, Loose Cannon. But what others may see as reckless is what Scott says is part of being a visionary leader.

"A speaker at our church observed that everybody wants to accomplish something significant in their life. But then they get into life and want to be comfortable. So they chase having a Volvo in the driveway rather than taking the risk to achieve something significant. It comes down to deciding: *Do I want to be significant, or do I want to just get through?* I want to do something of consequence, and I don't mean consequence in dollars. I mean consequence as in the legacy that I leave behind, and you can't do that by playing it safe."

ARC Healthcare

Healing is a calling, a truth made clear by the acts of heroism during the coronavirus pandemic by doctors and nurses on the frontline of the disease. Healthcare on the other hand is big business, comprised of a diverse array in industries including drug manufacturing, medical tools and equipment, healthcare facilities, and managed healthcare companies that together account for close to a fifth of the overall gross domestic product.

For Amanda Ratliff, building healthcare networks that navigate the complicated world of payor and provider contracting matters is both her business and her calling. To that end in 2012 she founded ARC Healthcare, which offers renegotiation support, provider data management, directory consulting, HSD tables, hospital contracting, single case agreement processing, negotiations, data analytics, and reporting among other services.

But ask Amanda what ARC's purpose is, and she says, "We help health plans fill their provider directory. The company's proprietary contracting software helps clients manage and develop their network so they can keep provider records for contracting and credentialing in one place with easy access. That's our core business in a nutshell."

All of which comes from Amanda's main passion: contracting and provider data maintenance. "I love to contract providers, groups, and hospitals to make sure the data collected in the process is correct, clean, valid, and complete. I'm really passionate about shuffling the data and data analytics around provider data."

Amanda says she's always had an analytical approach to things and admits to a touch of anal retentiveness. "I was always very precise about making sure everything was just perfect. Fat finger typos still drive me absolutely insane. I'm also very competitive. My mother jokes that when I was in elementary school, the gym coach would say to run one lap, and I would run twelve. I always wanted to be the best in whatever I did. And that hasn't changed because now I want to make sure that I'm providing the best quality in my industry. I guess you can say I've always been an entrepreneur at heart because wherever I was, I never wanted to be put in a box."

In retrospect it seems preordained that Amanda would end up somehow involved with healthcare although she initially fought it. "My mother was always in the healthcare space, and she always tried to nudge me toward healthcare. But I kept saying: *No, no; that's your thing, not mine.*"

Instead Amanda started her career in banking, which lasted almost five years. Then she went to work at Aetna in customer service and claims.

"Sure enough I ended up in healthcare," she says. "Your mother always knows you best."

After two years at Aetna, Amanda joined Molina, and during her six years there, she helped build one of the initial start-up plans in Ohio. "I really loved Molina's vibe," she says. "Their culture at that time was an old-school atmosphere where we were all family and looked out for one another."

Coming full circle, from there she went to work for her mother in 2012 at Access Advantage, providing overall healthcare service administration of the company's post-acute care (PAC) network. "I worked for my mother for a long time and tried to help grow her business in

Amanda Ratliff

and around nursing homes and home health. In the long-term care population, I noticed that people just weren't happy, whether it was nurses or those in the billing offices processing claims. I'd wonder: *Why is everybody so disgruntled or not enjoying their work?* I absolutely believe manual processes weigh on people. There's always this dread of: *Oh, no; I have to fill out this form and go back and check this box. And now I have to go over here and pull this file.* When I eventually decided it was time for me to spin off on my own, I wanted to be the one who was forward-thinking. I get that from my mother because she's a real go-getter. I found joy in my own work and wanted work to be fun for those who worked for me."

Amanda asks prospective workers where they want to be in five or ten years and what kind of work they like to do because putting your team somewhere that they're not happy is not a recipe for success.

"For example, I'm not outward focused. So at a conference you wouldn't find me in the forefront saying: *Hey, come talk to me.* I'm not that person. Now, there are people who would argue that from their perspective, I'm quite extroverted. But I'm naturally introverted, and I prefer being behind the scenes. So for me it's about finding out what people strive to do and where they want to be. I'm making sure that they are content in their job."

Amanda says she's a big believer of hiring people you know because they come with built-in trust. "I think when you build a business that's so personal, you have to bring on friends and people you can trust. I know some people disagree with that and some have criticized me about it, but to me it's meaningful trust. That's important for a stable foundation."

It was equally important for prospective employees, whether stranger or acquaintance, to understand Amanda's intended path. "As the company grew I would do the personnel interviews because I wanted people to hear my voice. I wanted people to see the vision and the passion and understand where I was trying to get to."

When it came to building the business, Amanda concentrated on providing the best service possible and let growth follow from that. "I never really focused on growing the business. I just wanted to invest in the bigger vision over the long haul. And once I started my own company, we really tried to mirror and mimic the family dynamic Molina was so good at, which is how we've developed our culture in the business."

That culture wasn't just about treating her team well. It was also about taking the time to establish relationships with all stakeholders and then treating them with courtesy and respect.

"Getting to where we are now, I always tried to stay abreast of what was happening in any market from an eagle's eye view of culture in how you treat people and how customers should be treated," Amanda says. "It's like the old saying: you can catch more bees with honey than vinegar. I grew up in the South, and it's really important to me to always say *Yes, ma'am* and *No, ma'am* and be respectful because at the end of the day, it all comes down to how you treat people."

Amanda points out that everybody has rough days where maybe your patience is short, or you might not be as considerate as you usually are. The difference is owning up to it.

"If you mess up, just say you're sorry. That goes a long way with people."

With an ever-growing population and aging of the baby boomers, healthcare is an ever-growing industry, meaning ever-growing amounts of documentation. Knowing how the drudgery of bloated paper pushing can wear staff down, Amanda sought a better, more efficient way.

"I always want to find the cleanest path of least resistance. Which way does the water fall, and how can I make it fall easier, faster, and more smoothly for everybody? So I've spent the last many years of my life chasing how to do it faster and better. I'm just compulsive by nature, so when I couldn't sleep at night, I'd Google to see who was doing what and how they were doing it."

But more than entrepreneurial OCD, insomnia, or her research skills, Amanda says the foundation of her company's success was her faith. "For me it's bracing myself on a firm foundation of biblical attitudes and the favor of God. I believe you need to have a Christ-like attitude in how you treat people in your culture. That's how I built my team. Then by the favor of God, we got blessed with a larger contract that was really meaningful, and I wanted to make sure that we did it well by growing to scale, getting all the communications on point, and having everybody in the right roles. Once all the ducks were in a row, then it was making sure I didn't fail because failure to me was not an option."

As the company continued to grow, Amanda delegated more of the hiring to Human Resources. But there was a disconnect.

"The HR team wasn't really focused on the way that I wanted to model things. They were putting price versus Christ in the center. And one thing that was really apparent to me was in order to fix what I think needs fixing, I had to put Christ in the center of my business. I think the way we live right now in our culture makes people shift around in their seats a little bit uncomfortably, so you need to be bold with it," she says. "I would rather fail at this one thing than forsake my own belief. I'd rather lose everything and look back and say was it a fun ride based on me putting Christ in the center than saying I didn't do that. So every day I'm going to put Christ in the center, and I'm going to follow the direction that He tells me. There's no doubt that He's guided me here. Every day I hear a word from him—*Go do this. Go talk to that person.* It almost seems like divine navigation."

Amanda lives out in the country and says she often spends time outside. One morning she was out doing yoga prayer as the sun was coming up.

"I'm sitting there in lotus position trying to figure out who my strongest leaders were who would help me build a solid foundation for the business so I could scale. Then God said: *Pick up these rocks.* So I did and arranged them in a circle in front of me. Then he said: *Pick up this one*, and it was shaped exactly like a mountain. Then he told me to try and stack them."

Amanda first tried balancing about eight rocks on top of one another, but they kept falling down. "I was getting frustrated because it wasn't working. So God said instead of trying to stack them all on top of each other, to go around the mountain. That worked. He told me exactly the ones that needed to go around me to create a sturdy base and then the ones that would stack on top. And as soon as I identified those people and put them in place, I heard him very clearly say: *You have now created this team that will carry you.* My team is rock solid."

When people come in to interview for a job, Amanda puts the company culture out front and center. "I tell people we pray, we laugh, and we cry together. Christ is very apparent here. I need to have very visible signs of Christ, such as crosses in the office and such. I want to forewarn them, so they know what they're stepping into."

She equates it to the lessons in Robin Sachs's book, *Get Off My Bus!* You need to make choices to ensure your passenger list is in concert with both your journey and destination.

Of course, not everybody is suited for or comfortable with the company's faith-based foundation.

"I've had some harsh things said to me," Amanda admits. "One person told me that I over-Jesusfied the office. It just didn't make sense to me. If you're somebody who really enjoys Christ in your life, how do you over-Jesusfy it? So I've had to swim upstream. But then I've always gone against the grain."

A company culture isn't only meant for inclusion; it can also be a template for determining what qualities you want in individuals or businesses you work with, such as integrity, honesty, and respectfulness. "If you're not on my bus as far as treating me and my team well, it's probably not going to work," Amanda says. "We need more unity in our culture. In my opinion God put us all here to work together cohesively."

That emphasis on treating others with respect is just one of the things that Amanda believes separate ARC from the competition. "Honesty, integrity, and being able to step back and say: *I feel proud of what I'm delivering.* I always try to put myself in my customers' shoes and think: *If I were on the receiving end of my service deliverable, would I be a happy customer? If I give my word, is there transparency? Can I feel right about what I'm billing, and what I'm saying or doing or how I'm delivering it?*

Amanda uses an analogy of choosing between an expensive designer shirt or a cheaper knockoff. Usually it's not an apples-to-apples comparison because you typically have to sacrifice quality for affordability.

"Well, I want to be the best-quality $40 shirt in the market," she says, acknowledging that her original *the more customers, the better* philosophy that helped grow the company, is evolving. "You get to the point where you have to decide if you even want some customers when they are running all over us or treating us unfairly. Business is all about partnerships; I provide a service you need, so let's work together to get there. But it's harder and harder to find real partnerships anymore."

In addition to ARC's culture and people, Amanda says the company's other superpower will be its IT technology. "You need all three to get a really great product. In my opinion healthcare can't be manual, and we can't be doing things by paper, so I'm deeply interested in cracking that egg. Making a lot of this electronic is my number one goal. But you can't forgo the people or the trust or the culture you have to achieve that."

In addition to IT playing a greater role, Amanda envisions other changes ARC will have to accommodate in the coming years. The first is an influx of new employees.

"God told me something a year-and-a-half ago I find interesting. He said we were going to grow sixteen rungs from where we were then. At first I wasn't sure what He was talking about, but then I started thinking about Jacob's ladder," she says, referring to a biblical story in Genesis about Jacob dreaming of a ladder leading to heaven. "I always have these moments where I can see God working. I thought He meant a linear rung, as in we were going to grow upward. There would be me at the top and then sixteen brackets down."

Amanda related this story to a new employee, who had a different take on the sixteen rungs. "He imagined his ladder laying horizontal along the side of his house because you can't grow your team so deep that you can't see what's happening. If I'm going to have multiple business lines, I shouldn't go any deeper than probably three to six leaders and staff with each line because I have to be able to pivot if I'm juggling different balls. I need the right leaders in the right places with the right teams below and have them all coming together for the greater purpose and their greater good."

She says it boils down to communication, uniformity, and reporting structures. "I'm trying to delve that out right now by determining what technology is the best to deliver so I can have a bird's eye view of it all at any given time. That will drive accountability. The patient populations and the needs are so great that it's almost unfathomable to see how much there is to tackle. I worry we're not going to have enough people going forward. We're working on a mobile app to engage our younger generation with our industry."

Amanda says even before COVID-19, people in healthcare seemed stretched and taxed. "I went to a conference, and one CEO was complaining that he was so busy he had to schedule when he went to the bathroom. He said: *If you're trying to sell me anything, you better make it five minutes or less.* There are so many people out there trying to sell, sell, sell. We need more thought leaders who are looking holistically at our industry instead of chasing bones that have already been chewed apart. I also think we have to find a way to break up some of the chaos and make it easier for everybody to work together, so we all have shade beneath the oak tree. I just want to work with everybody to provide the service that they need. We are coming to market with tools that will engage accountable care organizations (ACO), hospitals, larger health plans providers—the whole kit and caboodle."

ARC's IT tool is to streamline any paper processes. Earlier in her career, Amanda says she would travel the nation doing network development. She would hear from healthcare providers how challenging it was to keep up with the paperwork generated by having a dozen different health plans that they had to contract with while they serviced their patients and stayed current on billing and credentialing and whatever else.

"There has to be a better way to make it easier for everyone," Amanda says. "So right now we're looking for the right partners to pilot with and the right health plans that want to help us develop better software as a service processes. What do they need? What systems are they using? And how fast can we do it at the leanest cost?"

Amanda admits when she founded the company, building a new, proprietary software was not on her radar. "We did our business plan around the summer of 2019. I thought we'd just be a consulting service that could do X, Y, and Z and be done in ninety days. But it's become apparent that to have the IP side and the business side, you need the software because trying to get anywhere using manual systems in my opinion is not the right direction. So we've rebranded as ARC Healthcare."

In a bit of maternal irony, Amanda says her mom had been nudging her in that direction. "She always said: *Why don't you go into software tech?* I was resistant for a number of reasons. Number one, family is most important to me. I got married really young and had children young, so I never really had the time to finish college. I didn't know how to build code, I didn't have a business degree. But it turns out I'm good at finding the right people to fill in those gaps. That's why we all have to work together as a team. No one person is going to be good at everything; it's impossible."

Still, it took her a while to delegate responsibilities. "I was still processing payroll for fifty people and billing my own clients up until two or three months ago. I finally admitted I couldn't do it anymore. It wasn't going to get done timely or accurately, and I was hurting everybody. Again, it was about trust. The hardest part for me was releasing the financials and entrusting that to a CFO. But once I did, we moved forward."

Expanding the business from consulting to more full-service including IT, will be a delicate dance with clients because it will require an infrastructure realignment. "It's a little like shaking the tree a little bit. I'm trusting that between the way I'm leading, and the way the industry is moving will make people more open to the solutions we're offering."

If there is a life lesson she's learned through the process, Amanda says it's to follow your gut and don't listen to anybody that's going to tell you no. "I had a whole bunch of people telling me: *That's a stupid idea; don't do it. It's not going to work.* It's the fear of change and a lack of understanding. We need more people supporting and embracing one another, saying: *Yes, you can.* So find your cheerleaders and go for it. My husband has been a big cheerleader for me. If I come home discouraged, he reminds me giving up is not in our vocabulary. So I just continue to let God lead. He pushed me off the cliff, and I haven't fallen yet. When in doubt take the risk, and trust Him."

Regardless of the industry or size of the organization, information technology plays a critical role in the way companies do business, helping facilitate processes that help reduce costs, save time and resources, improve communication, boost performance, gain competitive advantages, and create innovative products and services. In short, IT has become the foundation to achieve strategic goals and sustainable success more efficiently.

And effectively harnessing the power of IT requires more than just technical know-how. There is no one-size-fits-all IT system or approach. There is an array of platforms, designs, alignments, technologies, and tools to choose from. While IT's diverse offerings are what make it so valuable, the possibilities can also be overwhelming, and without expert knowledge, nearly impossible to navigate. To leverage IT to its full potential usually requires enlisting a consulting company that oversees the management, implementation, deployment, and maintenance of an IT infrastructure.

"Most companies choose to work with consultants solely on the basis of *what* they do and *who* they've done work for," notes Ascent Solutions CEO J.D. Harris. "Brilliant and progressive companies, those that look at *how* a company operates where values, ethics, and relationships are at the core of what they do, along with world-class expertise, choose a different kind of consulting company."

A company like Ascent Solutions.

The definition of consulting is: *a field that focuses on advising organizations on how best to use information technology in achieving their business objectives*. But true IT consultancy is layered and complex. Effective and successful consulting entails a number of services that span numerous disciplines, including competitive analysis, development of an IT corporate strategy, implementation of IT systems, cybersecurity, and system management, among others.

On the Ascent Solutions' LinkedIn page, it notes: "Gone are the days when you could spend months planning, years implementing, and decades supporting an IT solution. Gone are the days of patience, second chances, and room for error. And gone are the days when you could choose your IT partnerships based on vendor speed, flexibility, talent, or price alone. You need it all."

That full-service purpose is what J. D. had in mind when he took over the company in 2014. "At Ascent, we're doing things differently," he says. "The four areas that we're in—productivity, cybersecurity, innovation, and managed services—are the fastest growing areas in IT. And within each one of those, we integrate cybersecurity. That's the big differentiator for us in terms of what we do. The cybersecurity practice is not just a standalone service line; it's actually integrated with everything else. So we can help companies from the onset be protected from one of the biggest threats to their future. That unique method of incorporating cybersecurity into every project has enabled Ascent to become the premier cloud and cybersecurity consulting organization and one of the most trusted companies in our industry. Nearly every Ascent customer has been a repeat customer. That's a track record we aspire to keep because it's unique in this industry."

J. D. has the perspective and experience to know, having been around the IT block more than a few times. While he acknowledges that his road to

J. D. Harris

Ascent followed a logical, professional progression, he adds with a laugh, "I can't say it was all on purpose. But I don't believe in accidents, only providence. So everything I've been able to accomplish has obviously been blessing after blessing."

He says his Christian faith has always been a guiding light for him, but at Ascent Solutions, "I've had the opportunity to truly lead with conviction, caring deeply for every single employee and customer in a deeper, more meaningful and lasting way."

His interest in and skill at technology was apparent early; he was still just a teenager when he got his first job as a programmer. Later he did consultant work to help pay for college at the University of Wisconsin, Eau Claire, where he earned degrees in information systems management and music.

"I was a bit of an odd duck," J. D. says. "It's not so uncommon for musicians to be in technology, but to have a degree in it is a little unusual."

Between his degree and hands-on IT experience, J. D. landed a job at Ernst & Young, at the time one of the so-called Big Six accounting and consulting firms in the world. He started there doing technical architecture—simply put, identifying IT needs and designing solutions—then quickly advanced through the ranks to an executive position, helping fix E&Y's largest global projects when they went off the rails. His work took him across the globe, and he lived for a while in France while helping Ernst & Young with their largest global project at the time. Despite being a job many IT experts would covet, J. D. couldn't ignore the itch to run his own company.

"It's something I'd wanted since I was a kid," he says. "In college I experimented with various start-ups, including launching a small advertising company with a buddy of mine. It was a tremendous failure, but it was worth a shot."

One thing J. D. learned was that he didn't have the right skill set yet. "Ernst and Young was a great firm. I loved it. They progressed me well. They were highly supportive. But I never learned how to actually run a business."

So when he was on the brink of a junior partnership, which J. D. noted meant being at the bottom rung of a new ladder, he changed direction and in the late 1990s left to become a partner at a small start-up. "I was the vice president of operations, running what we referred to at the time as our e-business practice. But I witnessed some unethical behavior there and decided I didn't want to be a party to that, so I left."

Over the next several years, J. D. worked at a number of companies, expanding his professional toolbox, learning different facets of operations, and building a strong opinion and understanding about how a business should—and should not—be run. In 2007 J. D. joined Kiva Systems in Boston, which Amazon bought for over $700 million.

"So that was a home run," he says. "When I left Kiva, though, I'd been doing start-ups for about fourteen years, and I was going to take a year off. I lasted long enough to take a trip with each one of my kids, which was super memorable and fun. Then a buddy who was a senior executive over at Microsoft asked if I wanted to come over and give him a hand in running a part of the country for Microsoft Consulting Services that was having a struggle. He was a partner back in my Ernst & Young days, so he knew my track record for fixing very complex organizations that were struggling. I ended up running the North Central US for Microsoft Consulting Services. I'm probably the only person who went to Microsoft to throttle back their career!"

He stayed for four years before the start-up itch returned. "Microsoft's an amazing company, but for me the land of start-ups and fast-growth firms is where I get my mojo from, where I wake up and am ready to go before the shower ever hits me in the face. And so I came to a hosting company called TekUplift as a partner and their CEO. And the first order of business was changing that God-awful name," he laughs.

After a year J. D. bought out the founders, sold off 95 percent of the company, which he says was failing, and with just a handful of staff rebranded Ascent Solutions as a consulting-only business focused on infrastructures such as cloud solutions, migrations, and strategic plans for large firms. Then Ascent forged a unique relationship with Microsoft.

"I built up my leadership team with mostly ex-Microsoft executives, who I felt could take a small company and help it exceed $100 million in revenue. When we had only twenty people, about six of them were executives. And that was on purpose," J. D. says. "I had a hunch that if we could create a consulting organization tailored to what Microsoft would love to see in a partner that we could be wildly successful. We have become one of Microsoft's most trusted partners in multiple sectors. In that ecosystem Microsoft has 450,000 partners globally, and we're in their top two hundred. So we have pretty aggressive goals; we want to be a $100 million company by 2023, and we're on track to do that and so much more. I'm not saying it's easy, but it means the opportunity is there, and we've got the team to do it. It's a group of people, mostly global experts in their areas. The best of the best in each category."

Along with good old-fashioned pounding the proverbial pavement, J. D. credits the partnership with Microsoft for helping Ascent grow its client base. "There was certainly a great deal of talking to friends in the industry—if nothing else, I'm very well connected in the IT community, and so is my leadership team. Even though Microsoft is very field sales driven, they need and love partners. If they have a really good partner they love to work with and have had success with—like Ascent—they will trust you with customer introductions, leads, and opportunities to work closely with them on products and competitive initiatives. We value relationships greatly, and Microsoft has been so great as a trusted partner of ours. So we don't do much advertising. All of our leads come either because of word of mouth or from Microsoft."

The delivery of goods or services is only one aspect of any company. The heart and soul of any business lie in its vision and culture, which Ascent has developed with intention and purpose. There's a reason J. D. often refers to himself as the chief culture officer. As such, it was particularly important to him that the company have a level playing field for employees.

"No politics, very little drama, and a huge dose of care for one another," he says, which includes how people are rewarded. He recalls how the start-ups he worked for prior to Microsoft had inequitable stock option plans for their employees.

"There were the haves and the have nots," J. D. explains. "At one company the people who had been there for twenty years barely got anything when the company sold, and then there were people who had joined the year prior that negotiated huge stock deals. It was very unfair and gross to me. So when I was at Microsoft, I thought: *If I could do it differently, I'm going to*. And I imagined what a cool program could look like. And it will hopefully handsomely reward everybody at Ascent if we have a transaction someday. And if we don't have a transaction and just have massive profitability, my hope is that it will handsomely reward them for that. So it's really fun, very different, and something that I want to write a book about someday as I think every company should set it up this way. To my knowledge, we're the only one."

J. D. says the stock plan isn't discussed prior to hiring. Once on board as a steward, the word Ascent uses for employees, the shares are given as a gift from J. D. and his wife, who are the largest shareholders in the company.

"I want people to understand that this is a family affair. We're bringing them into our family, even though we don't run it like a family-run company. This is definitely not a lifestyle company. This is a high-growth enterprise. We are all massive growth junkies here. If we're not growing—even if we were flat—we'd feel like we were dying. That being said, and contrary to popular belief, a company can have massive growth and have a family feel to it. That's what I want and what we're striving for at Ascent."

The next thing he wanted was to create a different kind of culture, one rooted partly in gratitude and faith. "First and foremost Ascent is really about God's blessing on this place and the hope and the trust that I have in His providence for what we're doing here and how we're doing it."

In his office is a painting that is a daily reminder of the culture's foundation. On the right side of the canvas are several large men and women, all wearing black. Their demeanor is smug and powerful and is intended to represent business as usual. And on the left side of the painting is a figure weak in stature, holding the cross of Christ, a group of people following behind him.

(Paintintg by fullofeyes.com)

"But they are also gravitating towards the central figure looming over both groups, which is the Lion of Judah or Jesus Christ," J. D. says. "It's meant to show a few things. One, if God is for us, who can be against us?

It's also a reminder to me that business can be done differently. Business doesn't have to be this dark environment; it doesn't have to be a dog-eat-dog world where everybody's looking out for themselves, grabbing for top dollar, playing politics, and all that garbage. If we absolutely look to Him, if we trust in Him, and if we do the right things, my hope is that He'll find favor in what we're doing, and people's lives will change forever. Yes, that could be monetarily, but more importantly I want all of us to be great stewards of every blessing in our lives—our families, our friends, our business relationships, and our material blessings. If that happens through Ascent, I'll be a happy man."

So far in just about every year of Ascent's existence, the company has doubled in size. "We don't know why God has us in this place at this time doing what we're doing. It's definitely for His purposes, not ours."

That said, in addition to the providence behind it, J. D. also attributes Ascent's culture to its core values, which were created collaboratively. Around 2016 a leadership team meeting was held off-site from the Ascent office. The six leaders were split up into three two-person breakout groups and were asked to write down who in the company they most admired. It couldn't be leadership team members; it had to be others in the company. And then they were asked to identify the attributes they most admired in those people.

When they started combining the lists, the first attribute that popped out was stewardship, which is why those who work at Ascent are called stewards and not employees. The second was passion, the third empathy, and the fourth was what J. D. calls *high candle power*—applied intelligence.

"How do you apply the God-given talent and knowledge that you have gained over the years towards a problem? And then we had this mishmash of stuff left over that we couldn't find a good uber category for it. Then one brave soul in my leadership team raised his hand. *Not to sound hokey, but I think what we're talking about is love.* And we all went: *Yeah, that does sound hokey, but you're right.* Then we tried to figure out how to define what we meant by love, and we couldn't."

J. D. opened the Bible app on his phone to see how scripture defined it. "We plagiarized the Bible," he jokes. "We are patient; we're kind. We don't envy, and we don't insist on our own way. We're not irritable, not resentful. We don't rejoice in wrongdoing; we rejoice in the truth."

When the core values were presented to the rest of the company, the response was resoundingly positive and enthusiastic. J. D. saw the deep irony in the response.

"What they didn't realize is we were just describing them, plain and simple, so of course they were going to like it. As incredible as our core values are, we don't have them on the website because we don't want them to be a marketing thing. We want to live them and protect them. Also, you can't truly understand them if you don't know how they were developed as our litmus test and as a tool to hold ourselves accountable."

J. D. says Ascent's core values are the most printed and used document in the company because they've become the litmus test for everything they do in business. "I use it before every board meeting to remind everyone that this meeting is going to be different from other boards they're on. If we ever have to let somebody go or make any other kind of tough business decisions, we use our core values to guide how to do it. There are so many decisions we think about where our core values guide us differently than in other companies I've been at. Take our supporting cast at home, for example, those people who allow us to do what we do with the passion and the power and the perseverance that we need to do this job well. Our core values dictate even how we honor them, so we decided to give our Ascent stewards their spouse's birthday off. That's one of myriad examples of our core values—real and living and active and vibrant—in action."

To help the company's many single parents, whose time is always stretched to the max, Ascent's *steward services captain* helps figure out ways to give them some time back. "He's like a concierge on steroids," J. D. explains. "He'll run errands, help you fix something at your house, he'll be at your house if there's a contractor arriving while you have to be at work. He's also a pilot and will fly stewards to and from regional meetings so they don't have to spend the night and can come home to be with their family. The steward services captain plays a variety of roles to help our people, but it all comes down to yet another way our core values drive what we do, how we do it, and for who."

Enhancing the lives of those at Ascent in this way is the fulfillment of a long-held goal that had been percolating in J. D.'s mind. "We were finally at a point where it made financial sense to do it, and it's super exciting. Again, you could look at it from the perspective that we're just providing nice benefits, but we look at it from a core value perspective and say: *Why wouldn't we do that?* It just makes sense."

It follows then that Ascent's core principles also play an integral role in the hiring process. When considering a prospective hire, there are at least five interviewers, one for each of Ascent's core values. After every interview loop, the interviewers get together with the recruiting team.

"We then go around the room, and everybody talks about their interview, both in general as well as from the core value that they were supposed to interview on. By the time that discussion's done, we have a general idea of whether or not somebody would be a good fit for the team. But then somebody from the recruiting team or I will ask one more question, and everybody has to say yes, or we don't hire the person. There can't be a no; there can't be a maybe."

That question is: *Would you be proud to have this person on your team?* J. D. acknowledges it comes down to a gut response.

"The cool kind of side effect of this process is that when you bring on somebody, the interview team is invested in helping them succeed. Obviously that alone doesn't ensure a successful hire, but we hardly have any turnover at our firm, and it all stems from hiring people that we're proud to be around."

He says he started using the question back in his Earst and Young days working on the project in France. "It's the single most profound, deeply visceral question that can be asked in business and if answered honestly and transparently, can set the stage for amazing team culture. Everyone is in it for each other, and that is the key to true success."

In the weeks that follow their hiring, J. D. has a conversation with the new steward to discuss Ascent's core values. "We talk about how to protect them. How they need to enrich them, how they need to hold themselves and others accountable for using our core values. It's a different lens to look through. It's not threatening; it's empowering. These core values are used over and over again, not for marketing or recruiting purposes, but within every process, every decision, and every element of Ascent's design, operation, and progression."

In 2020 the *Minneapolis Star Tribune* named Ascent Solutions #6 in its Top 150 Workplaces list and #1 in the entire state across all companies for its ethics and values. "This award has been the highest honor of my career, and something that my team should be especially proud of."

For the occasional person who's just not performing up to standards, termination is the last option at Ascent. "We always try to come alongside them first to try and help them. As long as they want to help themselves, we'll do everything we can until we can't anymore. This is the only company I've ever been at that as we've grown, the culture has gotten deeper and richer, not watered down and lost. That's because everybody here is all in for each other. The stewards here look out for others more than themselves. Again, that's a core value thing."

Another hallmark of Ascent is its agility. While the four main areas the company concentrates on—productivity, innovation, managed services, and cybersecurity—currently happen to be the fastest growth areas in IT, that will not likely always be the case.

"So if one of those areas starts to decline in popularity or importance, we have a methodology to incubate a brand-new service line or offering in thirty days," J. D. says. "We are always asking: *What are the newest things we need to look at? What's the next big thing that could take us to $100 million and beyond?* We're focused on what we're doing now, but we also leave ourselves open to what the art of the possible could produce. It's important that we don't get tied to: *We have to do this one thing* because what if customers decide they don't want that anymore? So we're constantly morphing because it's all about what our customers need and where we can be the most helpful to their businesses. That's our driving force."

From having worked for some of the largest and most influential companies in the world to shepherding his own company into a fast-growth, consulting force, J. D. has forged a professional path that has given him an entrepreneurial perspective a bit off the usual beaten track. So when offering words of wisdom to anyone looking to start their own start-up journey, he advises them to remember it's not about the founder; the spotlight should be on the company and the people in it.

"I know it sounds cliché, but within the company you need to surround yourself with people smarter than you. Even if it's costly, make a concerted effort to find those people. And then outside of the company, surround yourself with people smarter than you," he says. "Find people who have gone down the path before you like mentors and others you can go to as a CEO when you feel like there's nobody else you can talk to."

J. D. is quick to acknowledge that spouses and significant others are a critical support resource. "They can prop you up emotionally and be there to give you a much-needed hug or kick you in the rear and tell you to get over it and help you gain perspective," he says. "My wife, Tina, loves and supports me even with all of my craziness, all of my ambitions, and all of my faults. I couldn't do what I do without her. No way. She sends me off every morning at 5:00 a.m. with a cup of coffee and waves from the door until the garage door closes. Really, whose wife does that? It's amazing!"

While that kind of support from a spouse is important, they might not have the business background to offer sound advice on the professional end. "They probably have not been there and done that," J. D. says. "So finding the mentors, three or four wise individuals you can go to anytime and get advice from is critical. Sometimes mentors are there to commiserate, and sometimes they're there to push you back into the ring. Hearing someone say: *I've been there. I know what it feels like to lay in bed in the fetal position crying. And that's okay, but here is how you fix it. Now pick yourself up by your bootstraps and just get it done* is usually the impetus you need to keep going."

J. D. has been on both sides. He's had mentors, and now he mentors others. It's more than just paying it forward.

"I try to have a significant focus on giving back because honestly, I've been blessed so much by people massively smarter than me, who have taken me under their wing throughout my career and guided me. They have kicked my rear when I needed it. So I feel incredibly obligated to help wherever I can."

In addition to "official" mentoring, where people ask for a more formal arrangement, J. D. also enjoys talking to people on a more informal basis, getting together for breakfast or coffee. He also makes an effort to speak at a couple of universities a few times a year, and while there will meet with students one-on-one to have conversations about what being in business is really like.

"We all start out knowing very little to nothing about running a real-world business," he says. "The more you admit you don't know, the faster you're going to learn. And people will gravitate toward you if they see you're not so arrogant as to think you know it all. The more I've admitted that I know nothing, the more help, assistance, and knowledge I've gained. And I try to impress that on the next generation coming up. I love interacting with the up-and-coming business professionals. It's super satisfying and fun."

And that includes stewards at Ascent as well. J. D. says if someone were to say they were thinking of starting their own business, he'd be the first to congratulate them and offer his assistance where he can, sending them on their way. He'd never begrudge anyone their dream, in part because he still has more companies that he wants to start himself.

"I feel like I have four or five more of these in me before they bury me," he says. At the same time, he admits he doesn't have an exit strategy from Ascent per se. "I know we're probably headed towards a merger or acquisition transaction at some point. That's the likely outcome, and my team knows that. And I'll stick around as long as they need me, but there'll be a point where they don't, or I'm not the right person for the next stage of growth, and I hope I'm the first to identify that and let somebody better take the reins."

Retirement is not on J. D.'s radar. He's not one to live out his days tending a garden or playing golf. He leans more to the Warren Buffet school of keep on keeping on.

"I love, admire Warren Buffet. Years ago in a letter to shareholders, he lamented that one of his presidents was deciding to retire at seventy. He basically said: *I wish he wouldn't. I wish he would actually subscribe to my retirement plan, which is set for five years after I die, subject to change.* I love that. Yes, just keep going. I don't believe in work-life balance; I believe in work-life integration. You can do both well. I love my family to death, but I also love what I do so I love Mondays. And I hope everyone has a job they can say that about."

Brothers Paving & Concrete Corporation

All start-ups begin with a vision. For Paul Battista it was making Brothers Paving and Concrete Corporation the premier concrete and asphalt company in the DC Metro area, a one-stop-shop for contractors, developers, and property managers. How he achieved that goal is a classic American success story.

"In our first year, we did a little over $1 million in volume," Paul says. "Since then, armed with the best employees in the industry, we have successfully completed thousands of paving and concrete projects in the area. On the asphalt side we do all types of roadway milling, roadway paving, parking lot overlays, repairs, seal coating, crack fill, and striping. On the concrete side we do a lot of site concrete work and concrete removal and replacement, including bond release work."

Paul attributes the company's success to its attention to detail. "We self-perform 98 percent of what we do. We may bring in an occasional site partner to do some grading, but we normally do everything. We have employees who have been with us for thirty-plus years and understand the Brothers' way of doing business: We take time to do it right the first time. We exceed expectations. We keep our commitments. Above all else we value people."

That Paul would end up owning a contractor-related company was no surprise to anyone who knew him because he's been in the construction business all his working life.

"I started working for my father's homebuilding business while in high school," he says. "After graduating from college, I started building high-end custom houses during the boom of the 1980s. Contracting has basically been my life."

And to ensure the best possible products for its customers, Paul maintains continuous communication and solid relationships with his vendors. "I work very hard to partner with our suppliers. I will meet with them four or five times a year to make sure they know how we're doing and what improvements need to be made to help us meet our goals. I stress to them that we're all in this together," he explains. "We have great relationships with suppliers, and they're key to what we do here."

While the nuts and bolts of executing services are what builds a company's reputation and client base, the personal and professional growth of the founder/CEO is what helps establish a big picture strategy and productive company culture that is the foundation of sustainability. To that end, in 2018 Paul decided to go back to school—and in a big way.

"I also own a software company, and my partner in that business told me about a three-year program he was taking at Harvard," Paul explains. "It's an executive MBA equivalent—that's the term they let you use because the MBA is so sacred there. But when my partner encouraged me to apply, I told him: *I'll never get in.* I shared with him that decades ago, I applied to Harvard for law school, and they sent my application and $25 check back. So I knew I wasn't Harvard material."

But the partner brushed aside Paul's pessimism and insisted he come to Cambridge for a couple of days to audit some of the lectures. "He finally convinced me to apply, so I put the application together, and they interviewed me on my second day there. And I made it in—but barely," he says with a laugh. "The initial response was disbelief. Walking around the Harvard Business School (HBS) campus, you can feel the energy that comes out of the ground. You see the names on those buildings; you feel

Paul Battista

the history of the school. When I went to my very first lecture, I actually started to cry. I was so embarrassed I had to put my head down."

The program is primarily completed remotely, with participants doing case studies that each require about four hours of preparation. Participants also spend one month each year on campus, where they split up into groups for classwork and a living group of eight in the dorms.

"So you get there, check in, and they give you a coach for the first seventy-two hours because you have to form, storm, and norm as a group to perform," Paul says, explaining, "You get together—form—and work through all the bull. *Why does this guy sniffle every three seconds? I don't like the way this guy keeps going: HEY, HEY, HEY.* That's the storming part. Once you accept everybody's mannerisms, then you start to norm, which is when you all get along. And you need to do that within forty-eight hours because by then you have to perform in the groups. It's game on."

Most of the business owners Paul met in the program were running companies worth hundreds of millions. "In our dorm group there were five self-made billionaires who started with nothing. They were from all over the world, places like India, Brazil, and Lithuania. One owned a diamond mine, one was a unicorn in the education field, another ran the largest logistics company in Europe, and there was one of Mexico City's largest developers. I'm not a billion-dollar business CEO, I haven't experienced what they've experienced, and I don't have the wealth that they have, so it was a little intimidating at first. But no one talks about money. They're all about starting a business, scaling it, and selling it. When there, I'm with some of the sharpest minds in the world. And all my professors are on

Fortune 100 boards, including Google, General Motors, and Amazon."

A typical day on campus starts with getting up early because the study groups normally begin at 7:00 a.m. Participants work together on case studies for a couple of hours then attend a series of lectures.

"Sometimes there is so much homework you just lock yourself in your room at night," Paul says. "And that's what it's like for three and a half weeks. So you really have to disconnect from your own business to be fully engaged. The professors are brilliant but can be brutally honest and direct. They'll look at your case studies and notes and ask you what it says on page twenty-two. And if you can't answer, they'll say to everyone: *I don't think Paul's prepared. Is that fair to everybody else here who is prepared? Should we allow him to stay?* They'll call you out in two seconds. I'm not saying they're mean, but it really makes you perform at a whole other level."

The next challenge was applying what he had learned about building and scaling a business to his own company. "I came back from year one and completely restructured my business. In two years I literally doubled its size. But on top of that, margins increased at a multiple of five."

The course also helped Paul better identify his priorities, such as providing the best quality of life for his employees. "I have somebody cooking breakfast and lunch for everybody now. I have a former Mr. Universe come in twice a week to train everybody, and it's mandatory; if you're in the office, you have to attend these boot camp classes. We also put in a gym with treadmills and weights."

Three months into the new health regimen, Paul says his staff started seeing results in themselves and in their coworkers, which was an incentive to adopt an overall wellness lifestyle. "Even before we provided meals, people stopped ordering pizza for lunch in favor of things like grilled tuna salad," he recalls. "As everybody's mindset started changing about being healthier, they found they had more energy and were more productive because their brains got healthier."

Paul also started offering health insurance to all employees. "That's a huge financial investment, but I want everyone to know that health is important. Two years ago I'd have people come to me and say: *My wife is sick; I don't have the money to go to the doctor.* That's not right. I can't take out profits to go buy a boat. I need to make sure that our employees who are making things happen for the company are being taken care of. And if I do that, if I care about the quality of their life, they'll be here forever because they won't want to leave. One of my executives recently told me: *I was crying driving home yesterday. I love working here. I love what you've done. I love being part of this team. I'll go to the wall for you.*"

Offering full benefits wasn't an easy sell, but Paul explained to the other executives that besides creating continuity and helping maintain quality control, low churn saves the company money and resources—in other words, employee turnover is expensive.

"Training and grooming employees you can promote are crucial to companies. So I told the executive team that investment in healthcare is a win—not only for the employee but for Brothers."

Another innovation Paul has implemented is a recurring executive retreat to foster team building through training, presentations, exercises, and interaction. "We have hired one of the top job coaches out there to work with our executive team. She has done an amazing job helping us through the form, storm, and norm to perform process—own the process; own the outcome. She has coached each member of the executive team to new levels of leadership and accountability. Over the last two years, I transitioned our hierarchy from a wagon wheel with me in the middle to swim lanes in positioning our company to scale. I also hold weekly meetings to keep things on track."

While Paul says he always had the street smarts and ambition to start and build his company, advancing his education by learning from other CEOs and entrepreneurs gave him additional tools, structure, processes, and systems that have enabled him to maximize Brothers' potential.

"Usually when you're running a business, it's just you," Paul notes. "When you're worried about payroll, you can't go home and tell your wife because you don't want to worry her. If you lose a key employee and you're struggling to figure out how to replace them, all that emotion fills your head. There's always this certain level of pressure of what's coming at you next. With this program at HBS, I found myself in a room with other successful CEOs who knew exactly what I'd been through. It was mind-blowing; it was exhilarating."

Paul compares being around so many who share the experience of running a business to a pressure relief valve. "When I started HBS two years ago, all I really knew was the sweat off my back," Paul says. "We went from start-up to $22 million in 2008 before everything tanked during the recession, and then our revenue dropped 50 percent. Now we're approaching $50 million because I know what I'm doing. I know how to synergize a team. I've learned how to hold people accountable. I know how to set goals. We have metrics, we have balanced scorecards, we have key performance indicators—the same tools Fortune 500 companies have. It's all about developing a standard scale and technique for gathering data. All goals have to be measurable because without a metric you're never going to get there."

For all the accolades Brothers now enjoys, Paul's career path as a contractor didn't follow a particularly straight line. From working at his dad's small homebuilding business, Paul learned how to frame a house, install tile, and do plumbing, electrical, roofing, and carpentry trim while still in high school.

"I could do basically everything in the house except I never poured the concrete," Paul says. "But my college degree was in music; I did an internship with a symphony. I had a band. I had thoughts of going into music management and really wanted to go on the road with a band like The Police, Styx, or REO Speedwagon. But I was getting married and couldn't afford the low pay. Plus I knew I couldn't properly raise a family with that lifestyle, so my career in the music business never happened."

Paul's mother worked for Electronic Data Systems, and at her suggestion he applied for a job there. He was hired, made a left turn, and began working on computers as a systems engineer. The work was secure and lucrative; after four years he was making close to six figures. But Paul hated it. So when the planets aligned and he had a chance to get into home building, it was a sign from the universe.

"Because I was getting married, I built our first home," he says. "One day a guy knocked on our door and wanted to buy it. I sold it and paid off my school loans."

With the money left over, Paul bought a lot down the street and built another house that he says was the most expensive in the community. "I did it right. Everyone was telling me I'd never sell it. Well, I sold it before I had finished the exterior. From there I started a custom home business. At that age you're too stupid to have any fear; you just go for it. I built around thirty houses, including million-dollar homes in Northern Virginia. I did a home that had an indoor pool, one with an indoor ballet room."

But then the slow-moving train wreck that was the savings and loan crisis played havoc with the economy and ultimately put Paul's custom home company out of business. "You couldn't borrow ten cents to build a house," he says. "A good friend of mine owned a concrete company that nobody knew from week-to-week if it was going to make it. But he knew I had kids, so he hired me."

Paul worked there for a couple of months and then interviewed for a position at a paving company. "They hired me and said they would turn the business over to me if things went well. In five years I helped increased revenue from $1 million to $6 million. The owners were buying horse farms and yachts, and I was thinking: *I'm not getting any younger. What am I doing here?*"

When it turned out the owners had no intention of making good on their previous intimation of having Paul come on as a partner, he quit and started Brothers Paving with an acquaintance. "I still can't believe I did all that," Paul admits. "It was pretty gutsy. My partner helped with some of the seed money, and then I bought him out a few years later."

One of the things that attracted Paul to paving is that historically it tends to be recession-proof. After the economy torpedoed his custom home business, he wanted something with more solid footing.

"Almost everywhere you go on the planet, there are asphalt and concrete. You can either be on the new construction side or the maintenance side. We decided to focus on the maintenance side. It's like auto repair; even in a bad economy people might not be buying new, but they are still maintaining what they have. So if we do it right, we should do well during the good times and be able to ride out a bad economy."

One of the most difficult aspects of running a company is figuring out what it means to be a good leader. It's more than simply keeping the company financially afloat; it's getting the best out of everyone.

"At Harvard I listened to the other entrepreneurs talk about how to handle people issues," Paul says. "What do you do with your star player if they're incredibly difficult to work with? What was clear is that you cannot put the individual before the culture. That's guaranteed failure. Culture comes before the individual. Culture is what's happening when nobody is watching."

He self-deprecatingly says he was not always that great of a leader. "I was a good sales guy, so I knew the business would do okay. But I wasn't a solid leader. I didn't set clear boundaries because I was nervous about putting the culture before the individual. We had a common problem when you lead like that. The front of the house—sales—did not properly communicate with operations or accounting. You almost always had a contentious situation if you put everyone in the room together."

Paul says it made him wonder how professional sports coaches or managers handle dozens of star players' egos, where everybody thinks they're the horse pulling the cart. "It's nerve-wracking. Once I got to Harvard, I realized how you do it. It's crucial that you put the culture first. That might mean sacrificing a couple of individuals along the way, but there's no way you're going to grow or scale your company if the culture doesn't come before the individual. So when I came back after year one of the Harvard program, I put together an executive team, and we defined our culture. We began the process of being in a boat together, with everyone rowing in the same direction. The results were life-changing for each of us.

Morale improved, quality of work improved, processes were defined and adhered to. Top-line revenue increased, and profits soared."

According to Paul their culture is defined by giving back to the community, honesty, a love of doing the work they do, and valuing the people they work with. "It comes down to four core values: people, precision, partnerships, and professionalism. When I started putting our people first, everything else fell in line," he says. "It took a while, but people started to respectfully communicate with one another. People started to realize: *I'm not going to raise my voice because it's not allowed. And if I continue to raise my voice, I won't be here anymore—he means it.* We recently had fifteen people in the kitchen celebrating an employee's birthday. Everybody was happy and hugging. It was so unified. I was there thinking that two years ago, this never would have happened. When you have good communication, accountability with follow up, and give people an opportunity to have a voice, respect goes way up."

Another thing Paul says his company didn't have before his foray to Harvard was a detailed five-year plan. "During my second year at Harvard in 2019, one of my coaches asked me about my five-year plan, and I didn't have an answer. He asked me how big my market was. I had no idea. So I paid for an HBS MBA analysis and found out it's a billion-dollar market. So that enabled me to develop a plan to scale. We're still working on those numbers, but I'm looking for 10 to 20 percent growth every year for the next five years."

He also sees a market for verticals that in the future may include franchising and a solar division in addition to his current software company, www.Pavementsoft.com, which was originally developed by Paul and Shawn Boyce, a partner at Brothers. "We added a couple of amazing partners in the software company, and now it is now sold worldwide. The Brothers brand is really strong here," Paul says. "We have a presence in the homeowners' association market, so the solar would be easy to do if we do it right and have the right person running it. And coming out of Harvard, I have the self-confidence and knowledge to do it."

In addition to implementing that knowledge to his own business, Paul also passes it and his experiences forward to other up-and-coming entrepreneurs. "I have a friend who was getting ready to retire from the military, and he wanted to start a funeral home business. So I helped him put together a business plan and explained how starting a business works. You're the last person to get paid. When things aren't going well, you're not going to have money for your mortgage or maybe even groceries. If you don't have the stomach for all that, then forget it. Don't go down that road; you'll never survive. But if you do, then give it your all. If you can dream it, you can do it."

When Paul talks to college grads, he tells them there are two types of people in business. Those who sit at the base of a fruit tree and wait for overripe fruit to drop and hit the ground. It might be overripe or bruised, but it's safe and requires less effort to retrieve.

"But the entrepreneur who wants to change the world is going to climb that tree, crawl out onto the end of a shaky branch, and stretch as far as he can, almost to the brink of falling, to reach the sweetest fruit, the fruit closest to the sun," he says. "It's risky, even scary at times. Branches are going to break, and you're going to fall a few times and may even get hurt. But you will dust yourself off, recover, and start all over, climbing back to the upper, outer branches where the sweetest fruit is hanging. Why? Because to you it's worth it."

Paul notes that everybody wants the rewards of a successful business. "But do they really have the will to endure all that it takes to receive that reward? Most people don't. If you want to go for the sweetest fruit, it's going to take a strong will to win, the ability to manage risk, and some guts. If you're not interested in that, go get a job working in a cubicle. I've always been the dreamer. I think big, and I'm going for the sweetest fruit every time. And I'm the guy who will stop at almost nothing to get there."

In the earliest days of the auto industry, manufacturers sold their cars through a variety of platforms, including mail order, department stores, and traveling salesmen. But the primary model was direct to consumer sales. William E. Metzger from Detroit is often credited with founding the first independently owned United States car dealership in 1898. It was an idea that stuck.

As the car industry grew, the market matured, and the number of available makes and models increased. Dealerships evolved as well, offering additional services and creating a need for more efficient systems and processes. Before the digital age, that was basically limited to handwritten ledgers. Personal computers paved the way for more advanced databases and proprietary applications, such as DealerBuilt's full service, Windows-based LightYear dealer management system (DMS), which helps manage a dealership's enterprise, including accounting, customer management, finance and insurance, form printing, parts and vehicle inventory, service and parts departments, amongst other key systems.

DealerBuilt co-founder Michael Trasatti says, "It's a sophisticated system for a unique space. It's not something you can simply put together in a few months and expect to manage a dealership. Additionally, DealerBuilt has always had subscription-based licensing, typical for the industry now, though this was long before you saw a SaaS model."

Compared to other DMS, LightYear is unique because it's a true enterprise system, able to handle complex dealership groups under a single platform with a shared set of database files. It's also extremely scalable, able to work for dealerships large and small. Part of DealerBuilt's appeal is that clients retain full transparency and control over their data, so if a dealership has its own IT staff, they can write proprietary programs to integrate with the LightYear system.

"Dealers are seeking a DMS that is not just an operating system, but also an extension to their business," Michael explains. "LightYear is that extension, empowering dealers to make technology partner decisions to spur growth and meet the expectations of today's customers. Our DMS provides dealers a transparent way to communicate with their customers directly, such as texting, estimate signing on a digital phone or device, and mobile check-in. DealerBuilt helps our dealers stay ahead of the curve with a commonsense approach to integrating with third-party vendor partners by providing dealers with additional choices on how they wish to do business. Our DMS is also intuitive and one of the few enterprise solutions out there that is naturally graphical."

Competition in the dealership technology market is fierce, and client satisfaction is integral to success. Michael says to that end DealerBuilt continually reviews its clients' feedback and collaboratively works to continually improve LightYear so "our dealers are able to provide end-users with the best consumer experience in the industry."

In its first incarnation, DealerBuilt's LightYear DMS was a spreadsheet developed by John Hosmer, who ran a couple of family-owned dealerships in Mason City, Iowa, and was looking to create a better management tool to run the businesses more efficiently. It was an idea rooted in customer service and profitability.

"The more efficient the dealership," Michael says, "the more customers benefit and the better the operation."

Michael Trasatti

John and Michael met in 2008, and after a few meetings they formed DealerBuilt with a third partner, Frank Lucas, and together they enhanced John's original DMS into a scalable software platform designed to handle a much larger segment of the market, specifically the multi-rooftop dealership group. Today John remains focused on product and customers, Frank retired in 2019, and Michael runs the company, saying DealerBuilt is an enterprise he was practically born to run.

"I always tell people I was raised in the car business. My father opened a Lincoln-Mercury dealership the same year I was born, 1969. I grew up at the dealership during most summers, working in every aspect other than selling cars."

Michael and four of his six siblings followed in their father's CPA footsteps. "I got my degree in accounting because that was the thing to do in our family," he says. "But it did not appeal to me to end up being an accountant. What I gravitated towards were computers. It was a friend of mine that suggested I switch gears and get into software. After earning my accounting degree, I went back to school for a computer degree to ultimately work as a software developer."

One of his pet pastimes was writing various software programs for his father's dealership. "I always had this idea that you could make life better in automotive retail with technology. Back in 1994 my father handed me a book called *Customers for Life* by Carl Sewell. After reading the book, I wanted to write my own customer relationship management (CRM) program for the automotive space, which would have been revolutionary at that time. Unfortunately, I didn't know how to write software in a Windows programming environment and didn't have any real money behind the idea. We developed a few programs but eventually needed to find additional work, which landed me doing consulting and development work in Texas."

Then in 1997 the dealership purchased a DMS, CARMan, from a company called Dealer Solutions. Michael recalls, "It was written in a language I understood, and the software was supposed to provide flexibility and be easily extendable. I envisioned extending the system to do our own thing with it. Well, it didn't work," he says with a laugh. "We couldn't balance the books, couldn't close the month or send financial statements to the factory. After chatting with the people who had sold the system, I ended up spending two years consulting for Dealer Solutions in Houston, basically stabilizing the accounting application. I was essentially the fix-it guy, and I was good at it. The accounting module eventually became fully operational. ADP bought that company in 1999, and I stayed for several years working with ADP as a consultant, but with a twist."

ADP retired Dealer Solutions' product because they wanted to build an online version just like it. So Michael spent a couple of years developing a web-based app.

"I was a lead developer specializing in writing the accounting processes into the web version. For many reasons beyond this chapter, the project never made it out of quality control. ADP decided to switch gears again, and when they realized what it would take to build a next-generation DMS from scratch, they ultimately shut that down too."

Michael left ADP and the DMS space in 2004 in part because he wanted to stay closer to home. "I was traveling every week, which was becoming too cumbersome at that point as we were on our second child."

He took a stop-gap position as the chief information officer for a consumer finance company that needed a tech guy. "They got me off the road, though I knew I wasn't there for the long-term. The work was great but seemed it would be short-lived. I thought that at some point I would likely want to branch out from being a chief information officer." And he remained as bullish as ever on creating his dream DMS. "I thought: *There has to be somebody out there willing to put some dollars together to build a DMS. Better yet, I can find one that already exists and help revolutionize or evolve their DMS technology.*"

Michael tried to generate interest with investors but says the appetite wasn't there. "Then through luck, divine intervention, or whatever you want to call it, a mutual friend introduced Frank and me to John Hosmer, who had put together a nice DMS and started a small Midwest company called LightYear. He was burning candles at both ends by also running two dealerships. His existing partners were looking for an exit. They had a bit of shareholder fatigue and no vision of the future. John put feelers out that he was looking for someone to either take it over, partner with him, or buy the company from him."

John liked Michael's unique skill set—a CPA and software developer who knew the car business. After studying John's program, Michael believed there was a business to be had.

"I really came into the picture in 2007 to proliferate what John started. His DMS product had all the underpinnings to be a true enterprise solution and go after the market in a big way. With some assistance I wrote a business plan to secure investors—and then the economy collapsed. Of course that did not deter us. We simply rolled up our sleeves, redesigned the application ourselves to hit a larger target, rebranded the company, and then hit our network of dealers we thought would benefit from this revamped product. They agreed, and that's how we started DealerBuilt."

One of the first large dealership groups Michael pitched was Galpin Motors in 2008, which was the largest volume Ford dealer in the country.

Galpin was using the same CARMan DMS from Dealer Solutions that Michael's father used. When Michael worked for Dealer Solutions, he had gotten to know people at Galpin, including its business manager—and future DealerBuilt partner—Frank Lucas.

Fast forward to their pitch for LightYear: Galpin initially said no. "They were the only dealership still on CARMan because they didn't like any other solution out there in the market," Michael says. "They had a slew of other high-volume franchises, multiple rooftops, and they basically felt it was too risky to jeopardize the largest volume stores in the country and their billion-dollar enterprise on a no-name, unproven product from an upstart like DealerBuilt. However, we did secure their auto-sports location to run and operate our DMS."

Around that same time a dealer in Athens, Ohio, was looking for a new DMS that could effectively manage his multi-location dealer group. Michael says the dealer was intrigued by the idea of trying a new enterprise DMS at a competitive price point.

"Since I was looking for a pilot site to launch LightYear's newly configured enterprise solution, it was a win-win."

He reached out to Galpin's then business manager, Shelley Toomey, and told her what he had just done for the dealer in Ohio. "We took that new enterprise product and installed a copy at Galpin's Auto Sports location. I told her: *We created this enterprise solution I'd like you to take a look at. I know you guys are with one of our competitors; we just want to know if we're on the right track.*"

She was blown away, and from what Michael later heard, she went to the chief financial officer (CFO) and said: *This is the company we need to be doing business with. They have a product, quick to build out new features, and this system can handle our needs. These are the guys.*

"Eventually, we received a call the summer of 2008, and worked something out to install their entire organization in 2009."

That same year they also secured Performance Automotive Network. Michael says in that case the company loved everything about DealerBuilt; it came down to the dealer trusting him.

"The last meeting, which was going to make or break the deal, seemed to have little to do with the product. They just didn't know if they believed me and whether we could deliver for a group of their size. The question was: *Mike, how do we know that you're not going to leave us in the lurch if this thing doesn't work?* It became a really unique conversation about my track record, and about what our vision was, and what our goals were. That's why it's so hard breaking into this market. Several big-name companies have tried. Tremendous amounts of money have gone into trying to make a DMS like ours work, only to fail. It's a uniquely different space. Definitely not for the faint of heart, that is for sure."

Big clients, small clients, Michael says they grew DealerBuilt's business one customer at a time, giving each personalized care. "Regardless of the dealer's size, we had to get more intimate with the dealer. When you are trying to break into the market, there is little room for error, especially during the early days when our competitors—and likely much of the industry— certainly did not believe we would survive, and watched every move we made to pick up the pieces."

When DealerBuilt takes on a new client, the install and training teams spend months learning about the client's business, how it's run, programming the contract forms that are used to consummate a car sale, and understanding their existing needs to accommodate them. Michael says almost

every dealership has some type of DMS, so it's important to identify how to improve on what they already have in place.

"As part of the unhooking process, we need to convert the existing legacy data into our system. That is just one of many steps along the way in planning out an install, as they will always have variables. We also tailor each installation to the client's needs. Do we set up weekly install meetings? How much remote training can the client handle or desire? Same with the number of onsite setup and training days. We've had success with providing pre-go-live access to the system called a sandbox, where they can assimilate working with the application."

A new client's go-live day is typically a Monday, so the weekend immediately before, DealerBuilt's installers verify the remaining data and setup points, usually consisting of two to four trainers depending on the size of the client. Then after the switch is flipped Monday morning, they manage the rest of the training while the dealer is live and operating their dealership on the new LightYear DMS system.

With each new dealership, word-of-mouth becomes critical to DealerBuilt's future success. "Both during and after installation, we strive for dealers to talk about DealerBuilt to other dealers, to speak positively about our ability to deliver and do the right thing," Michael says. "We're pretty business-friendly. We don't have arduous contracts. If you want to add a new product and it doesn't work for your business, you can remove it. If the online videos don't provide the level of detail someone wants, we can provide onsite or personal training via a secure web session on the user's screen."

He notes that there's an increasing desire among dealers to get more bang for their technology investment buck. "Developing world-class products and co-innovating with forward-looking dealers go hand-in-hand. Beyond providing a user-friendly and scalable solution, perhaps our most important core competency is that we listen to our clients. So we're this breath of fresh air in our industry for dealers that traditionally haven't had a lot of flexibility within their DMS. And eventually we launched a national campaign that uniquely positioned ourselves as a flexible, enterprise-class DMS, evolving from what was once just a small, regional, Midwestern product."

When the company started, Michael was a typical entrepreneurial jack-of-all trades. He did installs, trained, hired, and rewrote conversion routines.

"Although I had the CEO title, there was nothing to be an executive over," he says with a laugh. "I carried the title, but you just do what needs to be done, whatever it takes. There was no guarantee of a salary, equity, or anything. All I had was the belief that if we created some value that resonated with the dealer body, then good things were going to happen. Initially all I cared about was getting someone to say: *These guys have a system, it has value, and it works*, along with paying the bills and not running out of reserves, of course."

Despite juggling due to limited resources, Michael still had to be confident in his ability to deliver on the corporate vision and to extend that vision to others working with him. "In my world, what I preach here is we want people who want to come to work at DealerBuilt because they believe in what we're doing and want to be a part of it. If you can provide a great place to work with meaningful, purposeful work, then you know you'll go to that next level."

Michael's goal is to accelerate DealerBuilt's growth beyond its current 25 percent year-to-year rate that DealerBuilt enjoyed the last several years. "Our industry is dynamic and is always changing," he says. "We're not a billion-dollar company; however, partnering with the right people and continuing to identify ways to scale without losing sight of our roots is going to get us there. As an entrepreneur you accept that the company will hit challenges and must be willing to evaluate skill sets, challenge the status quo, and be willing to make the tough calls to scale the business."

One of the challenges of growth is the realization that sometimes the people or processes that got you where you are today may not fit well with the future needs of the company. "In some cases your leaders or staff may question change or their own skill-sets and potentially lack the desire to make that leap to the next level," Michael says. "Any company that I know in growth mode will go through change management, and it's challenging on many levels. In the early days of starting a company, everyone works so closely together that you're fairly integrated with each other's lives. I view the entire growth lifecycle of a company as a testament to the achievement the existing team had. What they started—through all the challenges, late nights, making less than they could at other companies—has become something of real value for our clients. However, change is inevitable during a company's growth and can ultimately lead to new heights for everyone."

That lesson is just one of many Michael says he's learned about starting a company during his tenure at DealerBuilt. But the top of that list goes to the heart of being an entrepreneur.

"You have to love it. For me, that's number one. Love the business you're jumping into. I'm not talking about opening a business simply for passive income. I'm talking about creating something of your own; you have to love it enough so that no mistake you make along the way—and there are going to be many—interferes with your love and passion for the business. Just as important is your passion to be of value and service to your team and clients."

Acknowledging mistakes will help a company be more agile because it enables you to fail fast and pivot to a new strategy. "I didn't create the saying, but I use it all the time: *This company exists off of a string of mistakes and failures without losing enthusiasm.* Not everything you try will work, so don't hold on to it. Just admit mistakes and get past them. When we have failed slowly, it was painful. It's much better to rip the band-aid off fast and just move on."

Being stubborn could be the kiss of death for a start-up. Taking the attitude: *Damn it, I'm going to make this work* when it's clear that it's not going to, can kill you.

"You have to develop the ability to accept failure and then move on to find what does work. Understanding it's not going to be smooth sailing all the time will save a lot of time, energy, heartache, and money."

Another potential landmine to avoid for any company is acrimony among partners. Just as employees need to be a good fit with company culture, partners need to be a good fit with one another as far as vision and personality.

"When I pick partners, I try to envision the tough times, not the good times," Michael says. "How's that person going to interact when there are problems, which will inevitably happen. Are they going to bail on you? Are they going to judge you? Are you going to judge them? Or are you going to go: *Okay, that didn't work; back to the drawing board?*"

In Michael's view there are different types of partners. There are those who you team with to start a business, partners that have value and resources (financial, wisdom), and there are the important partnerships you create and nurture with clients and vendors. The key is that each partner has the other partner's best interest in mind.

"I don't care about the logistics. As long as I know there exists a mutual interest for each other's success, we're going to be okay," he says. "I have been fortunate to have successful partnerships. My partner John and I started DealerBuilt in 2008 and subsequently landed Galpin in 2009. In chatting with Galpin's CFO, we can reminisce about the struggles early on as a start-up trying to install such a large organization. However, in the end we truly feel each partner has benefited from the relationship, and that certainly makes you feel good about what you're doing when you can achieve that level of mutual success."

Specifically, the LightYear rollout at Galpin was not smooth; the system basically crashed the first week. "We worked our asses off to give them what they wanted," Michael says. "And in return they have continually opened doors for us and have become one of our biggest supporters."

DealerBuilt also has a new partner in ParkerGale Capital. The equity firm became a majority partner in February 2019 to provide resources the company needed to evolve and allow DealerBuilt to focus on its vision: *Evolving the DMS beyond a system of recordkeeping to a system of engagement by adding built-in customer experience tools that enable dealers to create sales and service experiences that exceed the expectations of today's tech-enabled consumers.*

"We wanted a partner who had a like-minded approach to our market, valued what we built, understood the complexities we face, and had similar values of the culture we worked hard to build. Our company enjoyed steady growth over the years through word-of-mouth, but we owe it to our current customers and staff to broaden our reach, fulfill their needs, and grow in a responsible way, while still providing great customer service and innovative solutions."

To achieve the company's ambitions, Michael's role has become more focused out of necessity. "There came a time when I realized that if I truly wanted to take this thing to its next level, there was no way I could continue to be the jack-of-all-trades," he says. "The company needed to function more autonomously. With resources provided by our ParkerGale partnership, we set out to find a leadership team that could allow me to truly transition from entrepreneur to CEO. As much as it can be rewarding to understand and exploit your strengths, you must understand your weaknesses and be okay with those as well. You also need to remain confident in your vision—no matter what. If you can do that, you'll put yourself in the position to achieve that next level sooner rather than later."

Fusion

Health care—the prevention, treatment, or curing of physical or mental injury, illness, condition, or disease—is one of the biggest industries on Earth. Such a behemoth generates an enormous amount of medical data and personal information that needs to be documented. Every doctor visit, insurance policy, blood analysis, diagnostic test, treatment order, and prescription written needs to be added to our medical record.

Not only do health care records detail an individual patient's history, not only do they enable effective communication with other health professionals for optimal patient care, they also allow for the sharing of information that can be crucial for, say, developing a vaccine against a raging virus causing a global pandemic. Over the years an electronic medical records industry has been established to provide private physicians, hospitals, and mainstream clinics in the United States with systems devoted to the creation, maintenance, and security of medical records. But there are still certain patients that remain underserved, especially those in correctional facilities.

Bryan Jakovcic believed there was an untapped opportunity in focusing on one niche target—patients in correctional facilities. "I realized I could make a difference in an underserved and underdeveloped market by providing quality, cutting-edge solutions. By having the patient population managed by our technology, we'd be able to provide timely information to one of the sickest patient populations in the country."

In 2006 Bryan founded Fusion Health, which provides electronic health records (EHR) software and related health information technology services to the corrections and rehabilitation industry as well as other government-run agencies. Recognized by *Inc. Magazine* as one of the fastest-growing private companies in the United States for four years running from 2017–2020, Fusion's software is used to manage the health of more than 350,000 incarcerated patients throughout the United States.

"We hire the best-of-the-best to keep doing what we do best: correctional EHR consulting, implementations, configurations, training, and support," Bryan says. "Our team is among the most experienced, most knowledgeable, and most innovative in the industry. We understand the challenges and constraints our customers face. We stay ahead of accreditation and certification trends and changes, new initiatives, and business opportunities to keep our customers informed, efficient, and forward-moving."

Prior to the early 1960s, medical records were handwritten on paper, making the sharing of information much more limited and storage much more cumbersome. The documentation system of records was not standardized, but it was basic: the patient's last name and either the last few digits of their social security number or some other simple numbering system. The files were placed on tall shelves, often on rollers, that took up an ever-increasing amount of space.

In the mid-1960s Lockheed came up with a game-changer: an electronic clinical information system. Other technology and engineering companies soon got on the electronic records bandwagon, developing systems for hospitals and universities. In the 1970s the US Department of Veterans Affairs adopted EHR to much fanfare. But private medical practices lagged in switching over to digital. To help nudge physicians along, in 2009 the US government enacted the Health Information Technology for Economic and Clinical Health (HITECH) Act, which was

Bryan Jakovcic

designed to encourage widespread adoption of EHR by offering physicians financial incentives. The goal was to modernize how the American healthcare system managed and shared clinical and administrative information to make it more time, cost, and security efficient.

By the time HITECH was passed, Fusion was already becoming the go-to company for correctional EHR implementation. "We earned the reputation early on of being able to provide a full-service solution within the time frame and budget needed," Bryan says. "As more and more correctional facilities began adopting EHR, Fusion became the consulting firm of choice in assisting dozens of county and state correctional healthcare agencies."

Today EHR is a secure and effective tool for maintaining a patient's healthcare data, for communicating with patients and other providers, and for supporting the patient-physician relationship. No more trying to decipher paper files, having to wait for faxed records, or searching for misplaced or misfiled paperwork.

Bryan says it's all about improving the quality of patient care, regardless of that patient's situation. "We take our consulting and corrections background and use our know-how in every implementation of our correctional EHR solution. And not only is Fusion one of the largest correctional EHR vendors in the industry, we are also a leader in the replacement of legacy EHR systems for correctional health agencies across the country."

Bryan's journey to the correctional EHR mountaintop wasn't linear, nor was he particularly single-minded. When looking at his business history, it's like Renaissance man on steroids, including time as a stockbroker, fireman, and computer tech. In his early twenties he also bought a neighborhood cigar store that remains a thriving enterprise.

"I've always been in business for myself," he says. "My dad was an entrepreneur. He came here from Croatia in the former Yugoslavia and did the whole American dream. He was always a hustler and literally quit his job when I was two months old, to go start one of his first businesses. So it was always instilled in me to go out there and do it yourself, failure or success."

Bryan attended a Catholic high school that charged students either $5 or three cans of food for admission to the school dances. He would go to a local warehouse and buy cases of canned goods at wholesale prices, then sell his classmates each can for a dollar apiece.

"They were still saving two dollars, and I was making 90 cents on each can—everybody won."

He also bought radar guns wholesale and sold them to classmates getting their driver's licenses at a lower cost than the big-box electronics stores. Bryan also had a side hustle building computers. By the time he went to college—the first in his family to do so—he was ready to tackle more ambitious enterprises.

"I went to Fordham University and got elected as freshman class president. I quickly realized that was nothing more than a gimmick for me to file paperwork for the university. So that was when Fusion originally started, although it's had more names than I can remember. I first called it Fusion Collegiate Intermediaries, which was a program I built to help automate the university's compliance filing for the Jeanne Clery Act."

The Clery Act required that campus crime statistics be available to students and their parents when considering a college or university. "Compliance allowed the universities to get money from the federal government," Bryan explains. "But in return the schools had to report how many thefts, rapes, burglaries, and whatever were occurring on the campus in a given month. My app digitally compiled the data as it happened, so I used that to help the university fill out the forms and submit them to the government. The app was nothing fancy, but I've always been interested in numbers and, frankly, in money, so I thought there had to be greater value in that app."

Bryan pitched his app to other universities, mostly the Ivy League schools, and says he got a lot of interest. But he was spending so much time promoting his app that he neglected going to class.

"Fordham had a strict attendance policy where it didn't matter what your GPA was. If you miss a certain number of classes unexcused, you failed. So I technically flunked out of Fordham. I went to the school president, who was using my app. And even though I had a good GPA, he said: *Sorry, policy is policy.* And that was it. So I went back home and got a swift ass-kicking from my mom."

His dad was more sanguine and suggested Bryan go talk to one of their neighbors who was an institutional trader in Midtown Manhattan. The neighbor let Bryan come in to see what the job was like, and it was love at first sight.

"It was all computers and money; I was like *this is great.*"

There was one catch. The neighbor was adamant Bryan would never be considered for a job without a college degree, which seriously raised his entrepreneurial hackles.

"My reaction was: *Well, screw that; you can't tell me what I can't do. I can achieve anything I put my mind to.* I talked to my parents and my dad, who is so helpless when it comes to technology that he still gets up to change the channel manually because he can't figure out the remote but knew business said: *You're just eighteen years old. Go to Wall Street and hand out your résumé.* So I literally was on the street handing out my résumé to anybody who had a decent suit on."

One of those men in a more-than-decent suit invited Bryan to his company, which was a boiler room where young, hungry traders made cold calls to sell stocks. "It was legit, but vicious. My boss was well known. He was a media personality, and he'd also been kicked off Wall Street twice and had started working under an alias."

Good times.

While the operation was legal, it was also ethically challenged. And the lifestyle was straight out of *Wolf of Wall Street*.

"These guys literally were full of testosterone, in at 6:00 a.m., out at 8:00 p.m., doing blow—party, party, party. One guy cleared $200,000 in a month, went out and bought a Lamborghini, and threw a crazy rooftop party. I woke up the next morning at my desk. I drank, but thank God I never got into anything else. After a year it started to hit me that industry wasn't what it was cracked up to be. The lifestyle was not me. I wanted to build something."

He left Wall Street, deciding he wanted to do Regulation D private placements, which allows smaller companies to raise capital through the sale of equity or debt securities without having to register their securities with the Security and Exchange Commission.

"That's where Fusion Collegiate Intermediaries became Fusion Capital," Bryan says. "And then the whole 2008 financial crisis started. And literally everything rapidly fell apart. That happened around the second week of September, a couple of days after the semester started at the universities. I remember running up to Seton Hall and being like: *Please, for the love of God, let me in*," he laughs.

And admissions did. So Bryan went back to school at Seton Hall and moved back with his parents. "I created another company called Uvisor, which leveraged data from the Department of Labor to create a parser.

Through that technology we were able to upload your résumé, look for keywords, and find jobs that matched."

Think eHarmony meets Monster. They unveiled the technology with much fanfare and even greater expectations at a big launch party in Silicon Valley. But things unraveled soon after.

"My partner did not come through," Bryan says. "I was actually paying him to come to work in our partnership. And my partner's brother wasn't able to deliver the investors as he had hoped. Plus, we were ahead of our time. So the venture was a huge failure. Fusion Capital was my one profitable business, so I was trying to figure out what to do with it next."

He also spent time as a volunteer firefighter. "I signed up on the day I turned eighteen," Bryan says. "It pissed off my parents hugely. I was with the Middletown Township Fire Department, which at the time was—and I believe it still is—the world's largest all-volunteer fire department. I just loved it and would camp out there most weekends. I like big machines, and I like craziness."

But it wasn't all action, all the time. He spent a lot of his time at the firehouse working on apps and day trading. "I was trying anything in finance because that's where I wanted to be but wasn't sure what exactly I was going to do. My father asked me if I wanted to take over his business, and I did not. It was his. He built the company. I needed to go figure out my own way."

Even though Bryan still had Uvisor and Fusion Capital, he was still looking for other ways to make money and scoured Craigslist looking for a gig. "I mean anything from fixing broken printers to whatever. Then one day I came across a job posting by a small correctional healthcare company in South Jersey seeking assistance in managing medical claims processing. I thought: *Hey, it deals with money. It's process, I'm kind of curious to see how all of this works.*"

Bryan set up and interview and met with the chief information officer, who was overwhelmed trying to help transform a growing company. "He had passed himself off as a programmer of sorts to help them revitalize their entire claims processing system but didn't know how what to look for. So by looking at the spreadsheets, I could see they were double paying claims left and right. In jails and prisons it's a very different system than on the outside; it's fairly complex," Bryan explains. "When we go to a doctor, we have our insurance cards. The inmates don't have insurance; the facilities are the insurance company, so they have pre-negotiated rates. They had no clue what they were paying out, and they were servicing something like eight jails in the state of New Jersey alone. So using Microsoft Access I created software for them called the Correctional Auditing and Billing System, or CABS. And that was my introduction into jails. That program is still being used out there in the field."

While Bryan was consulting with the healthcare company developing the program, they secured a new client, Newark, New Jersey's Essex County Correctional Facility, one of the largest and most populated jails in the country. "The facility used an EHR made by the GE Corporation. Part of the health care company's contract was to maintain and manage this EHR. Then the person who was managing it just up and quit."

The chief operating officer asked Bryan to fill in a couple of weeks until they got a replacement. "They were willing to pay my hourly consulting rate, so I was down with that."

Two weeks turned into a year and a half working at the Essex facility. Over that time Bryan learned the ins and outs of electronic health records, which included medical processes, procedures, and jargon, and developing content and reports.

"I was totally over my head," he admits. "While I was still there, a relatively young and healthy inmate died under suspicious circumstances, and a representative from the Department of Justice was brought in. They asked me if I could look at the database and see if this or that had happened? Long story short, by reviewing the audit logs, I found that somebody removed and modified the dead patient's charts before he died. It turned out a nurse had killed this inmate. I got an accolade from the Department of Justice for my efforts to help them. So that's where I first got my foot into electronic records."

Bryan says he eventually shut down Uvisor but still worked Fusion, which was making enough money that he could hire his brother Michael to work sales for him. "It was Michael who pushed me toward correctional work. I was still saying: *I want to be in finance. Why do I want to go to jails?*"

Michael saw that Bryan was in a perfect spot to capitalize on the work he was doing at Essex. "He told me: *You're building a name in corrections. Why don't we go to GE, since they don't know what the hell they're doing, and ask if we could sell their software too?* Of course he thought that because my brother wants to sell," he says with a laugh. "But we wound up approaching GE, which gave us exclusive rights, and we started selling that."

Fusion's first two clients were in Indiana and New York, and he quickly realized that small contracts would be difficult to scale. That gave him doubts about the entire venture. "I began to worry it was Uvisor all over again," Bryan says. "So I was just digging, digging for future opportunities, trying to figure out what we were missing when it came to the money. Then I stumbled across a bid from the state of Connecticut. The wording they used didn't match the keywords we'd been searching for."

The downside was the deadline for bidding was in two days. And the proposals required can run in the hundreds of pages. But for the opportunity to contract with an entire state was worth working around the clock to get the proposal in.

"We pulled the damn thing off and dropped it off in person with maybe a half-hour to spare," Bryan says. "So all the odds were against us. I knew it was a garbage proposal and thought there was no way we were going to get it. But we did. So I transitioned out of Essex jail back to the office—which was four-hundred-square-foot on top of a dance studio—and hired my third employee, Eli, to go to Essex and learn all about what an EHR is beyond the jail, and I was making a couple of bucks an hour off of him by contracting him out."

Eventually Fusion developed its own software program that went beyond what GE's platform offered. "One of the things that's made us so valuable is our understanding of workflows and our experience," Bryan says. "We develop our systems and our solutions to help cut costs. If you go back to CABS, that accounting software I built, that was designed to prevent duplication of claims, which ultimately cost the taxpayers more money. In addition to that our system analyzes patients. It can identify what care we can give now to prevent greater costs later by trending blood pressures, trending vitals, trending for chronic illnesses. So that's one of the things our software does very well. And that's a huge thing because when you look at inmates, it's the sickest of the sick. Jails are particularly more vulnerable to the spread of disease, such as COVID-19, because they admit and discharge inmates more frequently than a state prison."

After securing the Connecticut bid, the company grew steadily. Bryan estimates that Fusion software touches the lives of 350,000 inmates every day, which is about 20 percent of all inmates in the country. And unlike in the past when his start-ups were impacted by economic downturns, the corrections industry is essentially recession-proof. Nor does he worry about a smaller prison population.

"There's been an increased focus on the quality of care that inmates receive, and we're an essential component of that. So even if the inmate population goes down, the staff will be needed to support those inmates. And they're going to need a system like ours. They're not going cut costs by slashing health records."

In addition to growing through scale, Bryan is also looking for strategic vertical growth, such as Fusion's recent acquisition of Kalos, which develops custom management software for pharmacies located in correctional institutions and university health centers. "I always felt that the Kalos team would be a perfect fit in our vision, culture, and mission," Bryan says. "So when I was trying to figure out what was next, I set up a lunch with the owner where I asked if he'd ever considered selling his business. He was in sixties, and I knew his kids were not involved in the business. He initially said he planned to sell it to his employees, but in the end he sold to us. So now we've added a company I respected and looked up to that I never thought we'd be able to buy. It's just a beautiful thing and is the next stage of this company."

While his serendipitous introduction to the correctional EHR niche set Bryan up for a career in that industry, he admits mentally and emotionally resisting. It taught him a lesson he now passes on to others.

"Don't run away from what's in front of you. Up until recently, through most of this journey with Fusion, I did not accept that I was never going to be a financier. I went through all my mistakes, and Fusion was there for me, funding multiple mistakes. But I always kept telling myself: *What is this correctional health care thing?* So if you're not careful, you might not realize what you have right in front of you."

More than just providing advice, Bryan volunteers a lot of time for mentoring, "Because of how much Seton Hall embraced me and my entrepreneurialism while I was there, I'm on the board of directors for the business school now, and the Center for Entrepreneurial Studies, which gives me the chance to mentor some students. And many will say they want to own a business, but the truth is, being an entrepreneur is not for everybody. You need to be passionate about what you're getting into. You need to wake up every day and be happy about coming to work. You have to be willing to go all in. I've learned you can't start a business on the side. Your heart's never going to be there. You have to be persistent. I watched my friends going through college and sometimes think: *Holy shit, I'm not getting jobs, I'm just being this failure of an entrepreneur and trying all these things that are not working.* But you just have to keep going and trying."

Bryan also stresses the importance of practical business fundamentals, starting with getting the most out of your cash flow. "One of the things that my dad taught me was to borrow money when you *don't* need it. Go for your line of credit or loans when you have cash, not when you need it because no bank's going to loan you money when you need it."

Maintaining a healthy work environment is crucial. "Culture is huge here as you grow," Bryan says. "We've never had somebody leave Fusion under their own volition. Nobody has said: *I found a better opportunity. I found something that was a better fit. I found something that made me feel a larger sense of accomplishment.* And I'm very proud of that."

He admits one of the hardest aspects of owning a company is having to cut people loose, regardless of the situation. "And I've waited too long a few times to sever somebody because one bad apple really does impact the whole bunch. It can totally kill your business and work environment. Still, when we let someone go, it's done with a very heavy heart, but to build a culture of positivity and productivity, everybody needs to jive and work well together."

While hierarchy is important for organizational structure and efficiency, when it comes to management, Bryan is more egalitarian. "One of the things with our Fusion culture is that nobody sits on a pedestal. All my managers, myself included, are out in what we call the pit, consisting of about eighty workstations, which allows us to be engaged with all the employees and really connect with them. But I don't believe in micromanagement, either. That largely stems from the fact that we grew so quickly I couldn't personally be on top of everything; I had to delegate. I needed to entrust the capable people that I hired to take my ideas and run with them, to understand my vision and drink the Kool-Aid, if you will. And thanks to the culture we've built, they've all done a very good job at doing that, which is why we're the industry-leading company we are today."

It wasn't all that long ago that marketing a product or service meant literally knocking on doors to hawk your wares. Companies like Avon, Fuller Brush, and Electrolux became iconic brands thanks to their intrepid sales men and women who braved unfriendly dogs, annoyed residents, summer heat, winter cold, and constant rejection to earn their commissions.

But times changed, technology advanced, and today the Internet has increasingly become the preferred marketing frontier because nowhere can you reach as many people as quickly as you can online. The problem: anyone with a computer is vying for eyeballs and clicks, making the Internet a very crowded place. And with the digital age chipping away at our spans of attention, marketers need creative ways to attract potential clients. One of the most effective models—designed for tech companies like software developers—was to offer original content. *You give me your contact info and business specifics, and we'll give you this white paper to read.* The consumer gets pertinent and timely information, and the marketer gets data that helps them generate highly-qualified sales leads for their clientele.

Few are doing it better than Knowledge Hub Media, founded in 2009 by Paul Guenther. KHM has served hundreds of clients by leveraging syndication of white papers, webinars, and other content to generate call-ready leads—actually the preferred term today *demand generation* through content syndication, whether that be white papers, webinars, or business case studies among other things.

"We generate leads through promoting these white papers because people are interested in the topics," Paul explains. "There are a million different topics covered by white papers these days, and because we run promotions across most viable business verticals we don't just target IT people anymore; we target everybody: marketing professionals, HR executives, finance directors, operations managers, and more. We've built our audience up to about twenty-nine million unique business and IT professionals and decision-makers."

In addition to specialties that now include B2B lead generation, content syndication, social media marketing, branding, and email list rentals, KHM also provides micro-targeted demand generation campaigns that filters for specific job titles, company sizes, industries, and install bases across whatever geographic region requested, domestic and international.

Recognized as one of the top privately-owned fast-growth companies in the United States, KHM has received Inc. 5000 honors from *Inc.* magazine three years in a row (from 2015–2017), and in 2017 and 2018 was named one of the Best Entrepreneurial Companies in America with their inclusions on *Entrepreneur* magazine's prestigious Entrepreneur 360 list.

Jason Feifer, *Entrepreneur*'s editor-in-chief, noted that companies selected to the Entrepreneur 360 "are deemed successful not only by revenue numbers but by how well-rounded they are. The companies that make the list have pushed boundaries with their innovative ideas, fostered strong company cultures, impacted their communities for the better, and increased their brand awareness."

Not bad for a company that developed as a part-time side business.

After graduating from Penn State in 2006, Paul says he didn't really

Paul Guenther

know what industry he wanted to work in although he seemed destined to own his own company wherever he landed. "I'd been an entrepreneur my whole life," he notes. "I grew up right around the time that the Internet and e-commerce were starting to take off, and I began selling products online as early as the mid-1990s. I was self-taught in web development and knew how to build out good sites with strong but natural keyword saturation. One of my friends always jokes that we were the first people on eBay and PayPal. At the end of high school, I started a company where I sold botanicals like herbs, exotic extracts, resins and things like kava kava that you couldn't find in stores, which I would source from different wholesalers. That business carried me all through college."

Paul attended law school, but that experiment was short-lived. "I definitely wasn't ready for that," He took a full-time job with a large retail bank and realized that wasn't a good fit. "Then I went to another job and didn't like that one either," Paul laughs. "I definitely had job ADD for a long time, with six different jobs from 2006 to 2009, jobs you might have made a career out of if you stuck with them. But generally speaking I just had no interest."

Working for a B2B focused company specializing in lead generation finally got his undivided attention. Once he learned the process of the industry, he quit and started his own company. "Combining what I had learned with what I already knew about web development and promoting content online, which I'd been doing it since I was fourteen, I figured it would be pretty easy. The way I saw it, all I really needed was to find one consistent client, then I could bide my time and build things up from there."

Although Paul had enjoyed his time at the company he left, there was one tendency he observed that he made a point of not doing in his own business. "It quickly became evident at my old job that we were often over-promising and under-delivering, which I recognized early on was a huge pain point for many of our clients. For example, a salesperson would sell a campaign totaling three hundred leads over the course of three months, but then at the end of the ninety days, we would have only delivered some sixty-odd leads because given the campaign's stringent requirements we just weren't that efficient at generating highly-targeted leads. To me, clients seemed pretty put off by that. So my value proposition from day one was to be very conservative in my estimates of what I could do and to make sure that I delivered those campaigns in a timely fashion."

Paul named his company IT Knowledge Hub because the original focus was on the IT industry in general—basically anything technology-, computer-, or enterprise-software related. IT professionals would consume white papers supplied by companies like IBM, Dell, and Oracle about different solutions they had developed.

"It was B2B content syndication here," he says. "When someone registers for and reads a white paper it conveys a certain level of intent, that they are at least interested in the sponsor and the promoted solution. So rather than offering ungated white papers that visitors could just click on and instantly read, you add registration forms where people would first have to input their standard contact information as well as their company name, company size, industry, and business email address. Once registered they had immediate access to the white paper of interest and the user credentials necessary to come back and download other content with relative ease."

Someone simply registering for a white paper and downloading it doesn't equate to a lead, though. Each campaign has specific targeted criteria attached to the lead goal. So for example, if a company provides KHM with a white paper to promote, the goal might be to identify prospects who are at least at the IT director level, or in some cases even IT VPs—people with real decision-making and buying authority.

"Most of our clients are enterprise-sized companies, so they typically sell to other large companies because their technologies tend to be high-end, high-cost solutions," Paul says. "So they're looking for companies of a thousand or more employees. There might even be specific industries targeted; for example, they might have a product that's only suitable for the education industry. So to become a qualified lead, a registrant has to meet all the other criteria, and also have a .edu email address. You have all these filters in place to ensure that your client is getting highly-qualified leads—people who have the potential to buy within a specified timeframe and the decision-making authority to pull the trigger on large purchases."

As time went on Paul noticed technology companies weren't just targeting IT decision-makers and C-level executives. They were including Human Resources (HR) VPs who made purchasing decisions for HR management systems, benefits software packages, and all-inclusive solutions that companies had started using so employees could log in and view their paychecks, request paid time off, and more—all through a back-end platform.

"We changed the company name to Knowledge Hub Media because we realized there were a lot of technology solutions out there targeting more than just IT professionals, so we started to promote different types of offers through current and new client assets," Paul says. "The online presence has changed job functions dramatically. Titles used to be more simplistic like marketing director and VP of marketing. But now in addition to those, you are seeing titles like VP of demand generation or director of email marketing analytics. Everything is just much more refined now than it was even ten years ago."

Even though KHM is well-established, it doesn't mean they can just sit back and wait for clients to come calling.

"I wish it were that easy," Paul says. "Sometimes it does happen where companies will proactively contact us or reach out through social media, our PR and advertising forms, etc. But the majority of it is done via outbound efforts. We use tools like LinkedIn to find the right people at the right companies to contact about the solutions we offer, sending them individualized, targeted, and personalized emails in the hopes of setting up a phone meeting. Typically, these folks know exactly what service we're offering, because their job is to keep the lead pipeline full. Most of the big software companies have huge annual marketing budgets, so they have to spend the money one way or another. It's just a matter of convincing them that we're a good candidate; that we are a highly capable and experienced company they can effectively spend a portion of their budget on. After that it all comes down to metrics and return on investment (ROI)."

KHM's ideal prospective client is typically a technology or software company that sells enterprise level software and also has some sort of asset to leverage, meaning a white paper, a webinar, a case study, solutions, or even a report—something that can be used promotionally to generate leads for the company's brand and tech solutions.

"It's not like it used to be where companies were pigeon-holed into doing one thing; a lot of the companies we work with have a half dozen or more completely different solutions that target various elements of technology. And those are the clients we tend to work best with."

Paul says many of the companies they work with have contracts with ad agencies and so rather than working directly with the client, KHM works with the agency, which presents new opportunities. "Once you get in with a good agency and are performing well for one of their clients, the agency is more willing to reach out with other clients looking to engage in content syndication and demand generation. We get a lot of new clients that way, which is really a cool thing because it provides evidence that we are doing things effectively and driving ROI."

When he started the business, the majority of leads came through email marketing, which was essentially a numbers game. For one campaign you might send out 180,000 emails to get maybe 1500 people who would potentially register for and download the promoted asset.

"Of course the percentage of registrants who qualified as good leads was even smaller because naturally they didn't all meet all the campaign's filtering criteria," Paul says. "But email marketing was by far the main channel for generating leads."

Half the battle in those early days was ferreting out the email addresses of the people he wanted to contact. The other was working on a minimal budget. "Other than the money I spent on vast email lists of IT professionals to target, I started with essentially zero dollars," Paul says. "I didn't have anything. I used LinkedIn and other online tools to find clients. And fortunately when I did find them, I was able to sell and market well enough to bring many of them onboard."

And over the years doing business online became easier. "Now there are subscription services on the enterprise level where you can obtain a wealth of information on B2B companies, professionals, and decision makers."

As with most entrepreneurial decisions, there are both upsides and challenges. The upside of bootstrapping is that you can avoid accruing debt to investors, remain in complete control of your company, and grow the business at a speed you're comfortable with. It often also means being a one-person show for a while.

"For about the first three years, it was just me, and I did almost everything from my home office," Paul says. "All I needed was to buy a separate phone line and a fax line, so my initial overhead was very low."

Over time the company grew enough for Paul to bring in a couple of sales contractors to help with client acquisition and later client services and marketing employees to assist with ever-increasing workloads. But it wasn't a quick growth spurt; it was growth spread out over years that sometimes felt as if it was stuck in neutral.

"Four months after starting the company, I wasn't making the headway that I'd hoped to make," Paul says. He also learned a lesson that many entrepreneurs don't anticipate. "I also discovered that some companies don't exactly make a habit of paying their vendors on time, which in 2009 meant I wasn't generating the necessary cash flow to cover my living and business expenses."

So Paul took a web/development and SEO analyst position at a company that sold surgical instruments. "I worked there for about a year and learned a lot that was beneficial to my quest of taking Knowledge Hub to the next level. During that time I continued building my company on the side until I had enough consistent clients and the steady cash flow needed to quit my day job at the end of 2010."

While some entrepreneurs dream of securing venture capital mega money to be the next unicorn, most founders take a more methodical approach for both practical and philosophical reasons.

"I'm not someone who likes debt," Paul explains. "I paid off my student loan debt—and it was a lot—as quickly as I could. I don't like to owe money, so the idea of looking for investors or start-up capital was always out of the question for me."

Nor is Paul in a hurry to hand over partial control of his company in exchange for padding his bank account. "I've had quite a few offers from venture capitalists interested in acquiring a portion of the company and even a bunch offering us large loans, but it's just not something I'm interested in," he says. "I prefer doing it organically—slowly and steadily. Some might think that's a flaw—and it very well may be—but it's the way I tend to do things, and for the last ten years, it's worked."

Since the company's inception KHM has increased its annual revenue every year apart from 2016, when year-over-year sales were down just slightly from 2015. But that was an anomaly, and the company is approaching the 2020s enjoying steady growth and profitability.

"It's just a cool thing to know that you're doing business at an increasing level of efficiency year after year and without outside financing of any kind," Paul says.

As KHM grew so did the number of employees Paul needed, and four years into the business he traded his virtual home office for a sublet brick and mortar space. Since then he's upgraded a couple more times to accommodate his growing full-time staff. But Paul's not a proponent of the traditional model of having to spend forty hours a week in the company office.

Paul and his wife, Allison, with their son, Paul

"I'm all for people working remotely and teleworking because nobody wants to go to the office every day; I don't either," he readily admits. "So on Mondays and Fridays everyone is permitted to work from home."

On Tuesdays, Wednesdays, and Thursdays, employees are required to come in for four hours any time between 9:00 a.m. and 6:00 p.m. Paul says that time in the office is important for maintaining smooth operations. "In our business issues with targeting, campaign fulfillment, and miscommunication pop up all the time," he explains. "It's so much easier when everyone can communicate face-to-face for at least those few hours, because when you don't have that kind of access, you end up unnecessarily sending emails back and forth to solve simplistic problems. All in all everybody seems pretty happy with the work-life balance that we've achieved."

Maintaining a productive and copacetic company culture is one of the key responsibilities of any CEO, but there's a big learning curve between being an entrepreneur starting a business and being a CEO growing a company with all that entails. For many entrepreneurs it's a difficult transition, especially when you have investors itching to make a return on their money and the pressure is on to succeed quickly—another reason Paul is happy he took the slow and steady approach.

"I was fortunate I had the time to figure things out as I went along," he says, admitting, "In the beginning I really never intended to have any employees because I had no intention to scale the business up to anything extreme. I was satisfied with the way things were going. Now, I was younger too and wasn't really thinking about things the way I should have been," Paul laughs. "But for a long time my attitude was: *This is going well; the only people I have to worry about are the clients.* There was no stress and no responsibility for other people's livelihoods, which is why I never envisioned a full staff."

The universe had other ideas. A friend of Paul's, Anthony DiFilippo, who had worked in sales for a long time, asked if KHM was looking to hire. "If there was any type of employee I could use it was a salesperson," Paul says, "especially a good one like Anthony because it inevitably meant that a lot of new business was coming our way. And that's what happened. He came on, crushed it, and we secured several new clients. Then we recruited another killer salesperson in James Pastuf, and business increased yet again. After that I had to start bringing in additional staff members to help with everything else. The first was my brother, Chris Guenther, who was instrumental in taking on most of our client marketing and fulfilment operations."

Unlike the traditional sales model of commissions-only earnings, KHM's full-time sales people are paid salaries plus commissions —without the pressure of goals. "It's definitely a different kind of system when you compare it to what other companies are doing," Paul acknowledges. "But it works. I don't instill any sales goals whatsoever. There are no monthly, quarterly, or annual revenue quotas to chase after."

Instead, Paul tiers out the commissions based on the revenue booked that month, and every tier goes up a percentage point in commission, starting at 10 percent for the lowest threshold, which runs from $1 to $30,000 a month, meaning KHM's commission rate is actually above the industry average even at the low end. And it goes all the way up to 21 percent at the highest threshold.

"With the tiered commission approach, our sales people can make a lot more money any given month by simply bringing in one extra deal or increasing the volume of an existing one," Paul explains. "Usually my sales people are in the top three tiers, and some are consistently in the 21 percent tier just about every month. When you have it set up that way, I think it offsets the necessity for goals because you're motivating people with financial milestones rather than simply applying pressure to perform. And it also means I don't have to warn people that they're not hitting some arbitrary goal, which is traditionally accompanied by an implied threat to their employment if they don't turn things around. So I definitely think the structure of our commission plan makes things a lot less stressful for everyone involved."

With every industry looking for specific IT solutions and technology companies developing software and systems to fill those needs, KHM is positioned for long-term sustainability; however, that doesn't mean they have the luxury of settling into the status quo. Precisely because of the increasing diversity of IT solutions, Paul says the expectations of clients become more and more difficult to fulfill as KHM customers are increasingly looking for extremely niche leads, down to specific job titles, micro-geographic targets, account-based marketing, and buyer-intent data.

"We have what's called a BANT lead, which stands for *budget authority, need, and timeframe*. On the form are a series of questions such as: *What is your role in the decision-making process; is your company currently researching cloud security solutions; do you have a budget in place?* With some of our client campaigns, leads only qualify when the person answers these questions in a very specific way because they want a highly-qualified, sales-ready lead. There's also install base targeting. For example, there are companies that develop add-ons specifically for Microsoft Office 365. Understandably these types of clients tend to only target companies that use Office 365. So you're targeting based not only on the job role, company size, and industry but also install base intelligence."

Such deep dives have necessitated building a database that analyzes for patterns of consumer intent. For example, if three people from the same company download the same white paper and on the registration form indicated they are looking to make a purchasing decision within three months, that is a lead the client wants because that potential customer has intent to buy. To that end KHM has developed an intent analytics platform that as of mid-2019 had three hundred different intent topics and is continually growing.

"It will be a subscription-based model where clients can go in and quickly generate lists of companies that are showing intent to purchase the specific types of solutions they're selling," Paul says. "In addition to identifying the degree of intent, there's also a buying temperature component that will offer predictive insights on purchase time frames. If it's within thirty or even ninety days, that constitutes a high buying temperature."

The data KHM is using to develop the platform has been collected from a variety of sources, a big chunk stemming from internal demand generation efforts. As Paul notes, "We generate thousands and thousands of leads per month. Plus with the email marketing KHM engages in, we can follow people using landing page analytics, gaining insights into the types of content they are consuming after the fact. Then we also leverage traditional website analytics where we measure the types of content users are engaging with on a regular basis. Based on cookies and visitor IP addresses, we can often determine their companies and geolocation."

There is also *social listening* where KHM analyzes social media data across Twitter, LinkedIn, Facebook, etc., and provides insights about companies and their decision-makers based on the content and statuses they're posting.

"I think this platform is going to be a cool thing," Paul predicts. "And there seems to be a lot of interest about it among the clients I've already spoken with. If you can build a list of say eight hundred companies that are the right size, in the proper industries, and that have an interest in buying the solution you're selling, you can then use that list in an account-based marketing demand generation campaign."

Paul says account-based marketing (ABM), a B2B strategy that concentrates sales and marketing resources on a clearly defined set of target accounts within a market and employs personalized campaigns for each account, is a growing trend, one he believes KHM's intent platform will integrate well with. He also plans to back up that belief with hard data.

"We hope to engage in a couple of different case studies with clients where we will provide the intent data platform to them free of charge, hoping to get back as much information and data as possible in terms of performance. In other words how did this campaign perform using our intent data versus previous campaigns that did not leverage intent data? I hypothesize that campaigns are going to perform better across the board, generating higher-quality leads, and increasing overall ROI."

Looking back over KHM's first decade and the learning curve he had to navigate, Paul can offer some sound advice to future entrepreneurs beyond the rule to not over-promise and under-deliver.

"To me, if you're going to start a business and want the best chance for success, sell a product or service that carries a high margin," he says. "You want to continually research and invest time and money into finding ways to increase your margins even more over time—which is not as easy as it sounds. In some industries as companies get bigger, their margins thin out because of things like increased overhead, inefficient manufacturing processes, and a plethora of other factors. But in industries like ours it can be the opposite because you are continually evolving strategically and developing new tools to increase your efficiencies. You won't necessarily grow your margins dramatically overnight, but it's certainly better than diminishing returns."

He also urges start-up owners to keep their fixed costs as low as possible, both in the beginning and later on. "Even now we still use VoIP telephone lines instead of paying for an expensive business phone system," Paul says. "In reality most people don't like being called all that much anymore, especially from unknown numbers. You really only get on calls when they're scheduled, and most of the time you're using your cell phone anyway. So by making smart choices—even small ones—you can keep fixed costs to a minimum and spend your money on what really matters."

Lastly, Paul suggests resisting the pressure of approaching growth as a race; let it come organically. "Founders often think that they have to grow this much, this fast. They don't. Take the time to learn the industry and ramp up methodically. Building KHM was not stressful; it was fun, and I enjoyed it. And by the time I took on employees and became responsible for them, I was ready to handle that role too."

Paul's not claiming that jumping in full bore or taking VC money and being on the clock to generate returns sooner rather than later can't or doesn't work. "But I am saying that when you become a slave to growth, it changes the company culture, and I never wanted that. For me, being the tortoise was better than being the hare, and I suspect that's true for a lot of entrepreneurs, at least in the early going. But at the end of the day, there are no two companies alike, and that's ultimately what makes business and free enterprise so intriguing."

Paul at the office

The images have become increasingly commonplace. Under blood-orange skies, waves of flames consume vast swaths of land and turn homes and buildings to ash. In August of 2020 the Pine Gulch Fire became the largest wildfire in Colorado history. That same month more than two hundred thousand Californians were under evacuation orders because of wildfires. The Forest Service in Maine reported that by August, there had been more than 530 wildfires in 2020, compared to just 356 in all of 2019. These fires also endanger the long-term health of millions from breathing smoky air.

Data from the National Interagency Fire Center shows the threat of wildfires has steadily grown in the United States since the 1980s. Part of the reason is human encroachment. Developers are increasingly intruding into wildland areas to build housing communities, which increases both the likelihood of fires and their level of devastation. Another significant factor is climate change. Climate change causes forest fuels—the organic matter that burns and spreads wildfire—to be drier and more prone to ignition. A 2018 government report warned that the continued release of greenhouse gases from cars, factories, and other sources would make fires more frequent. And wildfires release a significant amount of CO_2 into the atmosphere, contributing to the climate change causing the increased fires to begin with.

Reversing climate change will not happen overnight, and people will continue to roll the dice to live in woodland areas. But what can be done

Steve Conboy

now is to minimize the property and environmental damage caused by fires. To that end Steve Conboy, founder of M-Fire Holdings, has developed products and systems that protect houses and commercial buildings from catching fire. Steve's Proactive Wildfire Defense System helps property owners defend their homes from wildfires. It's a sprinkler system installed on the roof as well as nearby slopes, and it sprays a special chemical combination from a tank over the house, landscaping, and nearby vegetation to prevent a fire from advancing. When it's time to evacuate, all the homeowner has to do is turn the system on, and all the growth around the house will get saturated with the product, which will linger for a month or two.

"It uses water as a delivery agent," Steve explains. "I created this system because I was tired of seeing so many people lose their homes. Now you have something to defend your property when a fire is calling on you. The chemicals clinging to the vegetation prevents the fire from advancing. And what sets this system apart is that it also supports root growth—with no clean up like the red fire retardants create.

M-Fire Holdings has started installing the proactive home defense systems in Southern California, but it's been a challenge to break through the red tape and status quo. "I've taken my system and done demonstrations at fire training academies in front of hundreds of fire officials, who are the biggest skeptics because they think they have seen it all," Steve says.

"When I showed them what happens when using my system during a wildfire burn or a wood frame building burn, their jaws all dropped. But then they all say the same thing: *Good luck getting upstairs.* It just seems that the people who are most impacted and the entities that are most impacted would be really interested in at least trying it out. You don't think homeowners would be interested in seeing a demonstration for a product that could cut their insurance rates?"

The point being a proactive system should remove the homeowner's threat and result in reduced premiums. But Steve says it's a battle getting people to pay attention and understand there is applied science today that can save communities from fires.

"Look at the way we defend ourselves from wildfires," he notes. "We hire thousands of young guys and give them a hand-held hoe to go and dig a firebreak, often too close to the fire itself, as shown by us recently losing several firefighters in the 2020 Northern California fires."

Steve recalls getting permission to give a demonstration at a controlled burn in Ventura County. He went out the day before the controlled burn to treat the hillside.

"I laid down giant letters cut out of plywood that said *Save Cali* and sprayed the dry vegetation sticking out of the plywood boards. Then we showed up the next day at eight o'clock in the morning, and all these young firefighters show up with hand-held hoes. All day long the fire chief has them digging fire breaks, checking their endurance."

At 4:30 p.m. when the wind started blowing, the chief lit the hill on fire to check Steve's firebreak. The minute the fire reached the dry vegetation and the plywood letters that were sprayed the day before, the fire went out, and the sprayed letters *Save Cali* appeared as everything else around it burned and turned black."

Steve recalls how the fire chief couldn't believe what he

witnessed, dropping fuel on the areas that didn't burn and lighting it again, only to see fire break put it right out.

"So I looked at all the young firefighters and said: *What would you rather fight a wildfire with a hoe or a backpack full of chemistry?* The answer was unanimous. They all yelled: *The backpack!*"

About a year and a half after Steve's demonstration, a major fire broke out in Ventura County. As the fire grew, so did Steve's frustration.

"The news reports were saying the fore was heading toward the 101 freeway, and everyone's worried: *Oh my God, what's going to happen if it jumps the 101?* Now, you had every fire resource we've got—planes, helicopters, everything. And still it jumped the freeway and took out more than five hundred houses. What I'm saying is forget the planes. That's a waste of resources, a waste of finances because by the time they drop a blob of fire retardant, go fill up again, and come back, the fire's advanced. Helicopters are a joke. They're coming with such a little amount of water. It's a visual for media."

For all the wildfire fighters' training, the terrain of many wildfires makes it difficult for crews to reach the front lines. "But if we had four-thousand-gallon tanker trucks that could spray three-hundred feet, we could design firebreak spraying where we know the fire is moving toward. I could spray a firebreak in fire season, and as long as it didn't rain, it would still be active a month later, clinging to vegetation without killing the vegetation."

Steve says M-Fire has also developed treated wood soil retention mulch. "Instead of blending the retention wood mulch with water, when it's blended with our fire inhibitor, it can last six months as a fire break on the side of roads used for wildfire exiting. All those country roads where people die in their cars trying to escape and evacuate could be widened with a fire-treated retention mulch that would last all during wildfire hot, dry months."

On one hand fire is fairly simple. Fire typically results from the right combination of heat, fuel, and oxygen—specifically, the chemical reaction between oxygen in the atmosphere and some sort of fuel that is heated to its ignition temperature. So in the case of a wildfire, the fuel is wood. The heat needed to ignite could be a match, lightning, something else that is already burning, such as the tree next door.

When the wood reaches about 300 degrees Fahrenheit, it ignites. Some of the decomposed material is released as volatile gases, including hydrogen, CO_2, and oxygen, which we see as smoke. Also released are free radicals, which are uncharged, very reactive, and short-lived molecules that are also produced during a fire. The rest of the burned material forms char, which is nearly pure carbon. The charcoal sold for backyard barbecues is essentially char—it's wood that has been commercially heated to remove nearly all the volatile gases to leave behind just the carbon. That's why charcoal burns with no smoke. Fire also produces ash, which is comprised of the unburnable minerals in the wood, such as calcium and potassium.

So when wood burns—whether as a wildfire or in a house fire—there are two reactions going on simultaneously. First the carbon in the char combines with oxygen, which is a slow reaction. Think of how long charcoal in a barbecue can stay hot. Second is the reaction causing the fuel to ignite and burn, which involved free radicals combining with oxygen in the air. Together those two reactions generate massive heat, which ignites more fuel. In other words the chemical reactions in fire are self-perpetuating. The heat of the flame itself brings more fuel tree wood to the ignition temperature, so the fire continues to burn and spread as long as there are more fuel and oxygen around it.

For Steve to make a product that would stop a fire in its tracks, he

focused on the role that the free radical hydrocarbon molecules H+, OH-, and O- play in sustaining the combustion phase of any fire.

"M-Fire Holdings' chemistry works by breaking the free radical chain in fire," Steve says. "Our technology captures those free radicals, breaking the chemical reaction, and suppressing the fire's strength and ability to advance. I could walk into a pool on fire with diesel fuel, and with a little canister of our product, I could put it out and not worry about it reigniting around me. The M-Fire system is the first simple, effective method to protect people and homes from wildfires and to make wood-framed buildings safer for occupants and firefighters. The chemistry that I'm using is not a phosphate, like what they drop out of the planes. I'm using tripotassium citrate, one of the few fully biodegradable and non-toxic flame retardants that support new growth.

Steve stays away from monoamine oxidases or diammonium phosphates, which is in the red retardant that planes drop on wildfires. While it can be effective, there is a distinct environmental risk associated with that type of retardant. According to AccuWeather, it can "kill fish and make a waterway toxic with ammonia and phosphate if dropped over or near an aquatic area."

Steve is also an advocate of the mass timber movement, which he says started in Europe and Asia, made its way into Canada, and now is being adopted in the United States. Steel and concrete, the traditional material to build larger buildings because of their load-bearing properties, are notorious for their large environmental footprints because steel and concrete production emits large quantities of carbon dioxide CO_2. But now mass timber—engineered wood used as structural components for buildings—is a growing trend. It's considered a long-term, durable product and a critical carbon storage tool that's cost-effective.

The carbon storage element is a big part of the interest in mass timber. Wood produced when trees grow consume CO_2, chemically locking it away. So long as the wood doesn't rot or burn, the CO_2 stays confined. Using wood as a building material keeps the carbon captured until the building is destroyed and the wood degrades. A 2014 study published in the Journal of Sustainable Forestry calculated that substituting wood for concrete and steel in building and bridge construction could reduce global CO_2 emissions by as much as 31 percent.

There are hurdles though. Many current building codes limit the use of wood in the construction of larger buildings, a historical remnant of nineteenth-century fires, such as in Chicago and San Francisco, when stick frame wooden buildings were common.

"Mass timber behaves differently," Steve explains. "Mass timber has a charring effect and is self-extinguishing. Fire prevention research and design have made mass timber more feasible. It can be engineered to last through a fire, with designs to have it last two or three hours so people can get out, and the fire can be extinguished. I also believe that mass timber structure is better at seismic activity and high winds than steel. It's renewable and sustainable because it's sequestering CO_2, and it's the future of housing to build with things that don't produce carbon. However, you have to make it safe, and you have to defend the carbon storage."

M-Fire Holdings' product can be used to treat the wood during construction as the building is going vertical. "I think this chemistry has defended ten buildings in Oakland for the biggest national builder. So if you can show people, you can convince them, but it's not easy. He notes that the issue is both a resistance to change and a need to update building codes. "When the code says that char engineering is all you need, builders aren't likely to do more than what they're told they have to do, right?"

Another benefit of M-Fire's system is that it also helps protect a city's water supply. "When homes are burning and firefighters are out there for two days with the hose trying to make sure it doesn't reignite, where do you think all those toxin runoffs are going? Into the water table. Instead of watering for forty-eight hours, you can spray our treated mulch over the top of a building, and it will shut the smoke down instantly, encapsulating the toxins from stormwater runoff so we don't destroy everybody's water table."

Steve's passion for the subject of carbon defending has led him to write a carbon tax credit bill he wanted added to legislation that set a goal for the United States to plant a trillion trees by 2050 to fight global warming. "Instead of cutting emissions, the plan intends to address climate change by having a trillion new trees suck carbon out of the air," he says. "Trees in the first ten years of their life sequester more CO_2 than they do over the next twenty years before it's harvested. But until they understand where trees would have the biggest impact, the job is only half done. Don't just plant trees in parks. If we plant trees in the Pacific Northwest where there are reforestation programs that support our demands for affordable housing, it will have a real positive impact. My carbon tax credit bill would reward builders that defend the carbon storage, and this would make renewable, sustainable ways of meeting housing demands even better as we build defended carbon storage banks."

The back end of that is then defending all the carbon sequestered in the trees so it's not released back into the environment during out of control wildfires, which brings us full circle to M-Fire Holdings' prevention system.

"There are solutions," he says. "There are always solutions. It's a matter of finding them and getting them to the people who can actually implement them."

Steve's passion for fire prevention was sown during his days as a carpenter at Local 940 in Brooklyn. "I worked on housing projects in Brooklyn and the Bronx built by Fred Trump," he says, referring to Donald Trump's father. "But it was so cold in the winter that I figured New York's a good place to be from, and I transferred to California in 1975 and worked framing the big housing booms."

From there Steve started working as a technical engineering representative in the lumber industry. "Then in 2008 I moved into fire science because I knew we had to do more to prevent damage to the environment, lost property, and civilian and firefighter deaths. The best way to do that to become a technologist and develop systems and products to eliminate fire's ability to advance on wood structures. Also, mold contamination can occur following a building fire, which presents a health danger."

The move to wildfire defense happened after Steve teamed up with a scientist in Malaysia. "He invented the inhibitors but knew he couldn't get

anywhere in the United States. So I started to blend his chemistries here in the United States then take them to American laboratories to get accreditation. Then it's no longer a Malaysian product, but an American one."

Steve's efforts to promote his product—and educate officials about wildfires—have taken him all the way to the federal government. "I'm trying to get in a meeting with the current administration because they're frustrated over the wildfire budget defense loss, but the president says all the wrong things about it when he says: *We're not managing the forests properly*. The forests that have died from beetle infestation actually need to burn."

He uses Yellowstone as an example of the integral role fire plays in keeping the environment healthy. In 1988 fires burned 1.4 million acres in the greater Yellowstone ecosystem, the result of extremely warm, dry, and windy weather. But according to the National Park Service, within a few years after the fire, "new vistas appear while the lush growth of new, young trees emerges from the burned ground. Today, decades after the 1988 fires, those young trees are renewed forests, once again filling in vistas. Some visitors still feel the Yellowstone they knew and loved is gone forever. But Yellowstone is not a museum—it is a functioning ecosystem in which fire plays a vital role. Some of the vegetation in the greater Yellowstone ecosystem has adapted to fire and, in some cases, is now dependent on it. Fire creates a landscape more diverse in age, which reduces the probability of disease or fire spreading through large areas."

Steve says that controlled burns in populated areas can also benefit homeowners. "Most of our property loss is coming from dry slope-side fires. Look at the 2017 Tubbs Fire in Santa Rosa. At the time it was the most destructive wildfire in California history, burning parts of Napa, Sonoma, and Lake counties, destroying close to three thousand homes. That was driven by dry, slope-side fuel. So we don't want to dump all our resources into cutting dead trees. Let Mother Nature deal with it. We need to get proactive around these old communities surrounded by wildland fire territories that homeowners have chosen to build in."

Controlled burns have long been employed by Native American tribes as a way to ameliorate wildfires, and Steve says his system can offer assurances for local residents who fear controlled burns may develop into an out of control inferno.

"I was invited to do a demo for the Rincon Fire Department in Arizona, which is a sovereign nation. The crew used a bulldozer to dig out all this native brush that they can't stop when it burns. The fire chief dumped it in a parking lot, a pile four feet high and thirty feet long, and said: *Defend that, and after lunch we'll come back and light it on fire.* So I sprayed it, and after lunch he lit it on fire, and it was raging—until it got to where I sprayed. Then it stopped dead, just like jumping off a cliff."

Steve says the system is easy to use because homeowners simply have to turn on their sprinklers. "If there is a wildfire in your area, engage the system the minute you get an evacuation order. Don't wait or it could be too late. The chemical is dispersed through the water sprinklers, so it saturates everything surrounding the house, creating a protective perimeter. And after the chemistry dries up, there's no cleanup. You might see it glisten on a building's wood-siding, but you don't have to wash it off. We need to evolve and utilize science. Just like engineers have evolved building codes to make homes and freeways safer from earthquakes, we need to make homes safer from fires through science. Between 2016 and 2019 we lost thirty thousand buildings to wildfires in California. It's crazy."

He also thinks it's crazy expecting firefighters to beat back a fire driven by a Santa Ana winds with a hose. "The gels don't work; the foams don't work. And they don't give you enough time to get it installed. The only time we call the plane in is when we've been beaten because it's so expensive, often running into the millions of dollars. Plus the phosphate coming down in blobs the way it does has an environmental impact. A system like M-Fire's is only common sense. Think about a place like Malibu. The officials there shouldn't want to be the definition of insanity by doing the same thing and expecting a different outcome. They shouldn't want to have to continually rebuild Malibu. Instead they should be open to new technologies that defend their city, their homes from the next fire that will happen at some point. If they did, Malibu could be a model city for the rest of the world."

Steve advocates moving forward with what he calls a balanced build. "Just like with a balanced diet where you can't just eat meat, you have to have some vegetables too. So we'll still use concrete footings in the ground, we'll still use steel. We've a lot of old infrastructure that has to be replaced, but at the same time we must use more renewable and sustainable materials and systems. We have to create a balanced build going forward because we can't continue to operate the way we have since the late 1800s."

He says we need to support those architects, builders, and even insurance providers that promote new, better, more sustainable, resilient ways to reduce loss while we reverse the damage done to this planet since the Industrial Revolution. "That is how we get to a balanced and sustainable build."

Steve believes we can have a real positive impact on reversing the damage to our planet by engaging in four sustainable practices. "We need to provide fire protection to defend the carbon stored in wood buildings, promote additional reforestation, invest in clean solar and wind energy, and provide better and faster ways to proactively defend all our structures and wildlands from fires to shut down greenhouse gas production from this source. Today it's my job to reduce all fire risk, so my grandchildren can live on a planet tomorrow that was as good as we once had it."

The first recorded use of a mirror on a car was in 1911 by racecar driver, Ray Harroun, during the inaugural Indianapolis 500. At that time drivers had to be accompanied by a spotter called the riding mechanic, whose job was to act as the eyes in the back of the driver's head. The riding mechanic let the driver know where the other cars were and whether it was safe to pass. Harroun figured if he could lighten the car's load by using a mirror to see the cars behind him and getting rid of the spotter, he could go faster. He admitted he got the idea after seeing a horse-drawn carriage using a mirror so the driver could see behind him.

Harroun won the race, but it would be ten years before Elmer Berger would patent the first commercial rearview mirror to manufacture them. He marketed the mirror as a *cop spotter*. It wasn't long before car manufacturers started making their own rearview mirrors, which were considered a luxury add on. That was especially true with side-view mirrors. But by the late 1960s, the development of multi-lane roads and highways made them a necessary safety feature. And for the next half-century, while their design might change, they would remain largely unchanged functionally—until the digital technology ushered in the next generation of vehicle mirrors.

One of the industry's innovators is Muth Mirror Systems, which manufacturers the patented Signal Mirror and is the leading supplier of mirror-based LED displays for blind spot detection (BSD), lane change assist, and many through-the glass mirror technologies and future active safety systems. Muth, based in Sheboygan, Wisconsin, has two corporate divisions that supply the original equipment manufacturers (OEMs) and aftermarket customers. The company's BSD active safety mirrors are used by more than forty vehicle brands around the world.

The family-owned business is currently run by Ken Muth, who has built on the legacy started by his grandfather, Ken, who founded the K. W. Muth Company in 1947 after serving in the Navy. In the age-old tradition of entrepreneurs, Ken—or Ki as the grandkids called him—started the enterprise in his grandmother's garage, where he developed a machine that prolonged the life of batteries using cut pieces of paper. He later turned the company into a wood-based manufacturer. K. W.'s son, Mike, graduated from Northwestern University in the mid-'60s and became president in 1972, again pivoting the business into a leading supplier of acoustical packing, door and headliner trims, carpeting, sun visors and vinyl floor mats for cars and trucks made by General Motors, Ford, and Chrysler. Mike changed directions again in 1990 when he sold the K. W. Muth Company.

"He sold because, like everything in automotive, it was going to get commoditized," Ken explains. "It was just a function of time. The automotive industry is incredibly challenging because it's so massive. There are a lot of competitors, and someone's always willing to underbid and undercut you if they don't have any new business available to them. My dad saw the commodity train coming, so he sold that business to a company called Masland, which was quickly acquired by Lear, which is still around."

The new Muth Mirrors Systems was a leaner company with a focus on high-tech innovation, developing cutting-edge LED technology such as its Signal Mirror. Ken admits becoming the third generation of Muths to lead the latest business incarnation at age thirty-seven hadn't been on his

Ken Muth

professional radar, until the unexpected death of his dad, Mike, in 2007 at the age of sixty-four put the company in jeopardy.

"Back then I was working on Wall Street as a sell-side research analyst," Ken says. "When Dad passed away, the company was in bankruptcy over an intellectual property lawsuit. Upon his death I became chairman and CEO as someone was going to have to make numerous hard decisions on the company's behalf."

According to court papers filed in Wisconsin District Court, in September 2006 Muth Mirror Systems sued Gentex for intellectual property infringement of the Signal Mirror. Gentex was embedding the Signal Mirror into its own auto-dimming mirror, which General Motors used for higher-end vehicles like Cadillacs and Escalades but weren't making royalty payments to Muth for the use of their technology.

Mike's attorneys stated intellectual property infringement cases can take years to litigate. Instead, they advised him to file bankruptcy.

"They told him it would be much quicker because the bankruptcy judge would make a decision probably within a few months," Ken says. "Because Muth was a private company going against a large public company with an exceptionally good balance sheet, my dad decided to put the company into bankruptcy. My grandfather had died several years earlier, but my grandma, Margaret Muth—who at the time was eighty-nine—was incredibly sharp. She exercised daily, drove a car, and lived on her own. In hindsight I think having to tell his mom he was going to take Muth Company into bankruptcy was the beginning of the end for my dad. It was an incredibly stressful time for him. He was a very proud man and was embarrassed by what he had to do strategically for the company, and all that stress just kept on mounting on him day in and day out."

In October 2007 the Chapter 11 bankruptcy judge ruled Gentex had indeed infringed on the patents and owed Muth Company $1.6 million. But there was a major caveat. The judge also ruled the Muth's patent was null and void, meaning it was open to the marketplace.

"That's the problem when you go to a bankruptcy court," Ken says. "The judge was not versed in intellectual property. He was a bankruptcy judge, so he doesn't deal with patents. Losing the patent stressed my dad out even more. To him it was a really big deal because he felt that without the patent, it was the end of the company. I feel the stress of the situation killed him."

Ken says it wasn't just his family that grieved the sudden loss of Mike Muth. "The entire city of Sheboygan was just upside down because it had lost one of their important civic leaders, who was a champion for the city."

At the time Ken was working at Robert W. Baird, an investment bank in Milwaukee, about an hour south of Sheboygan. "I was very skilled in finance, accounting, and forecasting, and I was not willing to just let this go. I thought: *Let me see what I can do with it.*"

Ken and his two sisters, Pam and Lynn, also helped his mom navigate life without her husband. "They were married forty-five years and had dated since grade school, so they were true soul mates," he says. "My parents were financially stable because my father had sold one of his previous Muth companies in 1990, but my mom didn't have any knowledge of their finances because my father took care of that. It took me about nine months to figure out all the accounts, which attorneys he was using for all his numerous business and personal activities and where all his investments were housed. My sisters were amazing; they stepped up and spent a lot of time with our mom as I was not available, working two jobs."

Of bigger concern was the financial health of Muth Mirror Systems. Ken says the K. W. Muth Company was highly successful under his father's leadership. But he found problems in the new venture.

"My dad had a lot of great ideas, took a lot of risks, and had a vision of how things should be. He really was a consummate entrepreneur. But with the new tech-based company and a new team of people, he didn't execute the details. I think what happened with Muth Mirror was, he came into a fair amount of wealth after he sold his old company in 1990, and while he liked the idea of starting a new company, he just wasn't as committed. My dad gave too much autonomy to his engineering team and really gave them complete leadership of the company. "

Ken acknowledges tech companies need to have talented engineers to grow and invent, but their specialty is creating technology. Engineers aren't equipped in the cost areas of finance, accounting, sales, marketing, and global supply chain.

"I quickly discovered costs were not detailed well," Ken says. "After I came to the company, I said: *Okay, we're selling this product for $10. How much does it cost to make?* And nobody could give me the answer. There were no Excel spreadsheets; there was no accounting of it. They said: *Well, this is what someone's going to pay for.* I explained I understood what the market was going to bear in cost of paying for it, but when you consider all the wages, all the 401ks, all the healthcare benefits, the building, the depreciation, and all the software you need—what does it cost to make the product? They had no idea."

That's when Ken realized they essentially had to rebuild the company against the backdrop of a coming recession. "At my day job as a Wall Street research analyst, we were writing about how bad the recession was going to be, so I was aware of what was coming. That enabled me to go into a faster plan of attack."

Ken anticipated that the Muth Company was going to be heavily impacted by the economic downturn because when money and credit are tight, people put off buying big-ticket items like new cars and trucks. He used the recession as a catalyst and driver to redo the entire organization. Ken identified two long-time employees who became critical partners: Jim Wong and Pat Miller. Right away Ken could tell that these two were who he could trust, work with, and learn from while putting in very long hours and starting to restructure the company. Jim was in charge of product engineering and operations, while Pat was intensely focused on sales and marketing. Both were loyal, highly talented, motivated, proactive, and cohorts to Ken.

"While the recession was genuinely bad, it was also true the company wasn't following best practices and hadn't been managed properly for probably a solid five years," Ken says. "When I came into the company, we had $7 million of debt, the company was losing money, and had very few customers. It was a tough scenario to be in for sure. I think one of the things we got right is we acted really fast and aggressively—speed as a strategy we like to say at Muth. Our revenue went from $15.8 million to $6.4 million, so we downsized the company and got our costs aligned with our rapidly shrinking revenue. We went from 129 employees to twenty-nine, sold off a building, sold unused land, and sold unused equipment to raise capital to survive and went from six divisions to two, needing extreme focus and operational simplicity. Then we waited about a year for the marketplace and the recession to bottom out."

With the patent gone, Ken had to decide the best way to move forward, both in the near and far term. The Signal Mirror had been in the marketplace for roughly fifteen years. When the company was doing $15 million-plus in revenue, 99.8 percent was Signal revenue.

"I went through all the documentation, talked to our engineers, and listened to everyone's ideas. The reality was we were down to one customer: General Motors. If there was no longer a patent, the pricing would be coming down fast, and any competitor could enter this market segment."

In Q1 2009, Muth's restructuring of facilities and personnel was complete, and the company made its first small monthly profit in July as well as for all 2009. When most of the automotive landscape was still in crisis mode, it was time for Muth to go on the offensive.

"Making that major product shift, we shut down the company's glass processing division, another hard but necessary decision to position the company for future success," Ken says. "We needed to go from a high fixed-cost model to a more flexible and variable cost model to free up capital. Instead of paying forty employees to make a piece of glass for $2.50, we were able to buy glass from overseas suppliers for $1.25 with no payroll or overhead and hold vendors accountable for bad parts versus us throwing away our scrap. It was a huge financial swing for the company."

Organization redesigns are never easy, especially when it entails coming out of formal bankruptcy as your reputation is broken in the marketplace. Beyond new systems, new products, new processes, and a new market strategy, it can be difficult to get employees on board.

"You have to find people with the right mentality, skill sets, and willingness to go on a new exploration with you and to face the challenges that are not going to be easy," Ken says. "We had some really talented young personnel, but when you're a lean company with less than thirty employees, you wear a lot of hats. My finance and accounting background made me interim CFO and IT manager. We upgraded all our IT infrastructure—storage, servers, routers, switches, computers, wireless phones—as technology yields leverage and employees enjoy those investments as it helps their productivity. Also, buying equipment in a recession saved us a lot of money. Then as you grow the income statement and can afford it, you hire employees and start delegating responsibilities. Mind you, I'd never run an automotive company and didn't have any contacts in the auto industry. That was where Pat Miller and Jim Wong were so valuable and stepped up big in time of need. They both had a *do anything to survive* attitude."

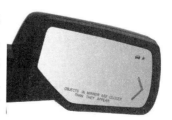

General Motors mirror shows Muth's combo of both Signal and LCA applications

Ken's finance and research background gave Muth Mirrors a broader, more global business perspective. "I spent a lot of time in China and Europe for my work at Robert Baird, so I appreciated different cultures. We had two sales guys in Detroit, and I spent my sales efforts in Japan, Europe, and later China."

One problem with selling to OEMs like General Motors, Ford, Honda, and Toyota, is that the sales cycle for a new product can take two to four years. "So in 2008 and 2009, I targeted the aftermarket segment with the signal to try and generate faster revenue with more trucks and off-road vehicles until our new blind spot detection product—a technology that was minuscule at the time—got into the OEM market."

The decision to target and pursue blind spot detection was based on Ken's experience as a research analyst, where he learned to identify trends. "If I wrote a research note on Cisco, thousands of people could read my report or I'd be asked to go on TV to talk about it and be grilled about my assumptions and stock picks. So by the time I joined Muth, I was very comfortable making forecasts and having opinions. I think I'm good at vision, assessing risks, and recognizing practical growth trends. I knew blind spot was absolutely going to hit, but OEM adoption and timing is unknown. So I told the team when timing was right, we were going to dump our signal product and revenue stream, and we were going all-in on blind spot detection. Again, when you're in a recession and losing money, you have to make tough choices quickly."

Muth's new BSD products didn't start gaining traction until 2012, five years after Ken joined the company. He explains that's how the automotive cycle works because cars are sourced and built well in advance of actual launch dates.

"For example, in 2020 we're working on 2023-24 model year vehicles. If you think about how the money cycle works, we have to invest the money for our engineering hours, our build of materials, and product validation certification well before revenues started to turn around and have to wait even longer to get paid. That's why we had to figure out how to connect the dots and the financials and liquidity because we knew we were going to start building a backlog of new wins, but we weren't going to get paid for two more years."

The critical piece of the rebuilding puzzle was coming out of bankruptcy quickly—not necessarily the easy way to go. "To take Muth out of the ashes and build it into something I didn't know was going to work, I wanted to do that with the highest integrity out there," Ken says. "I wanted to make sure that I could look all my customers and all my people and all the banks in the eye and say: *We're doing this right.*"

Ken took the company out of bankruptcy in March 2008, four months after the judge's rulings. The judge awarded Muth tortious interference, and Gentex paid $1.5 million. The two companies then signed a ten-year no lawsuit agreement. And as often happens in business, legal entanglements were compartmentalized from business. And today Gentex is one of Muth Mirror's top customers.

Ken says his father's half dozen investors—who were also his friends and local Sheboygan business associates—had invested in Muth at a $10 million valuation. When Ken was navigating through the recession, he estimates the company was worth maybe $2 million.

"I gave them all a $10 million valuation to make them whole," he says. "It took me time, but slowly over the next five years, I paid the banks back $7 million plus all their interest and all vendors got paid. No one lost money investing in my dad's company that went bankrupt, which I think is a big deal when you're setting the stage for how to rebuild something. Also, it got all the stock back into the Muth family as well as employees."

The first investor Ken paid back was Magna, one of the world's largest automotive suppliers with about $40 billion in annual revenue. Even though the company had written the loan off years before, he felt it was critical to make good on their investment.

"Coming from a financial background, I viewed the world differently from my dad as far as how money works, which is why I wired them $1 million within forty-eight hours of getting the money from Gentex. Magna had a behemoth stretch over all the countries in the world, with 180 facilities and 300,000 employees. If I didn't do right by them, they could tarnish me and wipe me off the planet pretty quickly with their scale and size. But today it is one of our best customers."

After two years of working two full-time jobs at Muth and Baird during the recession, Ken says he finally felt comfortable to leave his day job in late 2009 after Toyota placed a significant order. "I'd been over there seven or eight times promoting our product because at that point they'd never seen blind spot detection mirrors. We were the first one out of the block with a LED-based mirror BSD, so we had first-mover advantage. The Toyota order came in October 2009, I gave my notice at Baird at the end of January 2010, and started at Muth full-time in March."

Throughout his process of guiding Muth Company through a recession and new business direction, Ken's wife, Kate, was his rock. He says the company's turnaround would not have been possible without her support and devotion.

"She knew that when my dad died and I stepped in, our family's life would change. No matter how hard it was on her and how it impacted her life, she was very supportive and essentially became a solo parent to raised Michael, Libby, and Patrick for more than three years while I was working two full-time jobs, seven days a week. I would get home from traveling at 10:00 p.m., go to the basement and work with Jim until 3:00 or 4:00 a.m., then be back at Baird by 7:00 a.m."

Beyond the sheer physical challenge of juggling two careers, Ken also had to overcome a more subtle obstacle—expectations. While he was stepping into his father's role, he wouldn't be following in his footsteps. Even though he was his father's son, they were different personalities.

"My dad was a very large figure in Sheboygan County," Ken says. "He was like the mayor of Sheboygan. He loved this city, was passionate about it. He grew up here, went to high school here, and married his high school sweetheart, Jan Cerull, here. My dad was extremely outgoing and would go to events all over Sheboygan County. I'm not the same Sheboygan cheerleader, if you will. My mom and my sisters still live in Sheboygan, but I live in Milwaukee and make a fifty-minute commute every day."

Because their styles were so different, one of the hardest challenges for Ken when he took over as full-time CEO was developing a new culture away from his dad's formidable shadow. "The culture was the hardest thing to change here because my dad was so flamboyant and exuded such a strong personality. My style is to lead by example via work ethic, make data driven decisions, have financial discipline and make tough operational decisions. I'm the polar opposite of my father's leadership style."

While Ken remains bullish on advanced safety features on vehicles as a practical product target, one technology he isn't sold on is autonomous driving. "Look at the global supply chain of automotive suppliers, and they've probably spent collectively upwards of $20 billion on autonomous driving. And there are still no autonomous cars on the road. I would never be comfortable spending $100 million on a technology I don't believe in. But I do believe in vehicle safety. And if you look at JD Power and Associates and all the research reports that have been published, what consumers care about when they buy their next car are the safety features on it. Nobody asks: *What's the autonomous capability of this car?*"

Looking into the future, Ken says now that the company has grown, he wants to develop in-house technologies and look for strategic acquisitions, both domestic and international. But he notes that anything developed now wouldn't be on a car probably until 2025. Even so, Muth's blind spot technology has not come close to reaching its full potential.

"Blind spot detection is only used on about 15 percent of cars in North America, 6 percent of cars in Europe, and only on about 1 percent of cars in China, which is the biggest auto market in the world. So when we look at complementary technologies, I want something that's practical, that I believe in, and that is at less than a 10 to 15 percent take rate so it gives me that strong upside. Those are the products we want to look at."

In March 2016 Greenbriar Equity Group acquired 60 percent of Muth Mirror. While still very confident in the company's outlook, Ken did not want to make the same mistakes that his dad had by letting a company and industry put so much stress on his employees, his family, and himself that it jeopardized everyone's health. Ken says the transaction was a huge financial success for all stockholders, and the satisfaction of turning nothing into a financial triumph gave everyone involved enormous pride, great stories, and lifelong satisfaction.

When asked what piece of advice he'd give to a fellow entrepreneur just starting out, Ken doesn't hesitate to put knowledge front and center. "Do research and then more research because in the end it can save you both time and a lot of money. Before you spend any money, become an expert on your market and on every aspect of your product."

Ken sets aside Fridays for what he calls revenue and research. "I research my industry, my customers, and my competitors to figure out how I can bring more revenue into my company through the research that I gather. Spending that time gives me extreme focus to contemplate my vision of what to do with the dollars and resources we have available. And feeling you're an expert also gives you added confidence."

The final piece of the leadership puzzle is discipline. Ken believes it's something all great entrepreneurs practice.

"When you're an entrepreneur, yes, you have to take chances, and you have to take risk, but you must also be disciplined. Don't just say: *Here's $500,000; go spend it.* Be disciplined about where you're going to allocate those dollars and allocate your time, and it will serve you well through both good times and challenging times."

Ken's favorite quote he operates by is from Thomas Edison. "Vision without execution is hallucination."

Thanks to a variety of wildly popular television series such as *CSI, Dexter, and Bones*, even the most science-challenged among us are familiar with forensics, at least in relation to the part it plays in murder trials. But the specialty of forensics, which is defined as *scientific tests, methods, or techniques used or applied in the investigation and establishment of facts or evidence in a court of law*, applies to more than just homicides. Forensics play an integral role in bringing a spectrum of environmental, IT, and white-collar criminals to justice. Perhaps no specialty has been associated with as many high-profile litigations as forensic accounting, which was front and center in some of the most infamous tales of financial wrongdoing, including the Enron scandal and Bernie Madoff's conviction. It also helps courts adjudicate high-stakes divorces and Corporate America navigate big-money mergers and acquisitions.

As Jeff Neumeister describes, "Forensic accounting is the investigative area of accounting. It's like *CSI,* but instead of blood and bodies, it's documents and financials."

He certainly would know. Jeff has spent most of his nearly twenty-year career specializing in forensic accounting and has provided support and expert testimony in cases involving partnership disputes, fraud, income support calculations, lost earnings, and family law, among other litigations for established organizations, start-ups, holding entities, high-net-worth individuals, and middle-market companies, both directly and through their retained counsel. Jeff's reputation has made him a sought-after expert, and his business achievements have won numerous accolades, including the San Fernando Valley Business Journal naming him 2019's Accountant of the Year. He was also one of the National Association of Certified Valuators and Analysts' 40 under 40.

While examples of forensic accounting can be found as far back as ancient Egypt, its first notable use in the United States occurred when the Internal Revenue Service assigned a team of accountants to comb through Al Capone's finances. American Prohibition G-Man, Eliot Ness, might not have been able to stop the notorious gangster, but the IRS helped send Capone to prison in 1931 for tax fraud after he failed to declare the income from bootlegging and other criminal businesses.

Although the term *forensic accounting* wasn't coined until the 1940s, Jeff notes it has been around as long as merchants have been keeping books. "But once there was a label attached to that kind of investigative activity, services surrounding it became more structured. By the 1990s and particularly in the 2000s, forensic accounting really took shape with the slew of financial scandals that happened during that time at WorldCom, MCI, and Enron. That's when it became a critical specialty in the industry."

In 2017 Jeff founded Neumeister & Associates, a full-service accounting firm that specializes in forensic accounting and consulting services for clients in a range of industries including insurance, manufacturing, entertainment, pharmaceuticals, technology, health care, distribution, and finance. Based in Burbank, California, the company's services include commercial damage calculations, fraud investigations, family law matters, business valuations, and litigation support, in addition to more traditional CPA services.

"Most fraud occurs in relatively plain sight," Jeff says. "People

Jeff Neumeister

typically don't try to hide it. It's just that nobody is looking for it or understands to find it. That lack of oversight is how a fraud or misappropriation can go unknown for weeks, months, even years. We provide that essential oversight."

With a knack for even the most complex accounting problems and cases, it may seem like Jeff was born with a ledger and calculator in hand, but his first dream job during his grade school years was to become an archeologist, an aspiration fueled by *Indiana Jones*.

"Of course later on I realized no, that wasn't my ideal career path," he says with a laugh. "I went to college figuring I'd do something in business, but what exactly that would be, I had no idea. I liked computers and knew a little bit of coding, so I took an undergrad program in business information technology."

For the required business courses, students had the option of different tracks, including marketing, management, and accounting. Jeff says he assumed accounting and math were essentially the same thing,

"I liked math and was good at it, so I did the math-accounting track. When I graduated with my bachelor's and was out in the world looking for a position, I applied to accounting firms because I had taken so many accounting courses. Lo and behold, I got hired by a firm that specializes in forensic accounting. I didn't know what that was, had never heard the term, and never took classes in it. I quickly understood it was the investigative arm of accounting devoted to piecing together puzzles where the puzzle pieces are upside down, and there is no image on a box for reference. I fell in love with the challenge because I enjoy getting outside of my comfort zone. Over the next few years, I realized I wanted to continue my career as a forensic specialist."

Jeff explains that in the private sector, sometimes they were engaged to just calculate damages or prepare schedules. Most of the time forensic engagements are in the context of active litigation when a plaintiff sues a defendant in civil court. He says criminal cases are their own distinct animal, in a league of their own; usually the only people who work in criminal investigations tend to be in some type of law enforcement as such agencies have their own in-house forensic accountants.

"So most forensic accountants in the civil spaces are hired when Company A sues Company B for contractual breach, or when Partner A sues Partner B for embezzlement. Because it's often in the context of litigation, there's always a good chance you'll be pulled in and designated an expert witness."

Jeff says the objective nature of numbers helped quell his nerves the first time he testified as an expert witness. "Numbers are what they are. I'm not giving an opinion about whether a blue wall is painted indigo or navy. With some witnesses there's a lot of subjectivity involved, but five-plus-five will always equal ten. Though because it's a court situation, there is still a little anxiety being in that type of high stakes environment. You just have to remind yourself that when it comes to serving as an expert witness, the job of the opposing counsel is to catch you in a lie or mistake, to confuse you, and to make you appear non-credible to the jury. It becomes a game of wits to some degree, so you have to be extremely mindful of exactly how they ask a question, and to only answer the specific question they ask."

For example, if asked: *Do you know what time it is?* the correct answer is simply: *Yes.* Expert witnesses are taught not to add unasked information, such as: *Yes, it's two o'clock.*

"Being that precise can frustrate attorneys," Jeff notes. "But it also prevents you from playing in their game. that's one reason court testimony can take so long."

Jeff stayed at his first job for three years, developing a solid foundation for his future in forensics. He then went on to work for a number of different firms holding down various positions, including as an adjunct college professor teaching accounting. In 2017 he made the entrepreneurial leap to start his own company.

"It was prompted by a couple of different things," he says. "I'd reached that point in my career where I knew my stuff. I had aggregated a slew of credentials and graduate degrees underneath my belt. I had also developed a plethora of sources. Those milestones coupled with getting offered a full-time position as chair of the accounting program at Woodbury University, it was just the perfect concatenation of events."

Jeff notes that being a full-time department chair in a university is not full-time in terms of real-world hours. "We're talking maybe ten to fifteen hours a week. But having the foundation of the skill set, the referral sources, the contacts, and having this salaried position on the side through the university, along with knowing I would have the time to build my own practice, fueled me to make the decision to open my own shop."

Despite his years as an accounting professional and teacher, Jeff admits the process of building a business proved far more involved than he anticipated. "It is definitely more time-intensive, costly, and stressful than I ever expected. Becoming a partner in a preexisting firm is significantly less involved than building something from the ground up. There was no staff, no equipment, no clients—not even a logo. It was just me and what I brought to the table. It took a lot of grit to get the business to the point where it is today."

One of the more challenging aspects was finding a balance between providing pro bono services to prospective clients to show value versus doing the minimum to sustain a growing business.

"When you're starting out with no client base, you basically take whatever you can get," Jeff says. "And some clients had the tendency to want a lot for free because they didn't really understand the value we could bring to them when it came to professional services. It's much different than going to the store and comparing one speaker system to another by looking at the specs, listening to them, and seeing the price difference. Professional services are far more intangible, more abstract in some respects, so not everyone could really differentiate and understand the value proposition difference between the next company and us. So there were many times when we'd do a $20,000 consulting project and only bill $5,000 for it."

Several times during those early days, Jeff ended up actually losing money on a consultation because the fee didn't cover his employees' payroll and other overhead. But he considered it the cost of securing the company's foundation by building a strong client base—by all means available.

"Attending conferences, speaking at conferences, writing a book, holding lecture series, visiting prospective clients, tapping referral sources, lunch meeting after lunch meeting after lunch meeting, print advertising, online advertising, SEO—every single marketing avenue you can name, I did it," Jeff says.

After just three years, Neumeister & Associates passed the seven-figure gross mark, which many entrepreneurs would consider having turned a growth corner. But Jeff's ambitions are more expansive.

"My metric for establishing what I consider turning a corner is based on where I want the firm to be in the next five- or ten-year period. So while we absolutely have a solid client base now, for me we're still turning the corner because I'm aiming for the firm to reach eight figures, which will probably take a couple more years. I'm very good at scaling a business. In the book I wrote earlier this year, one of the chapters was entirely about scaling a business for sustained growth and what it takes to do that."

He says it comes down to a mindset and understanding the target growth you're reaching for. "There's a huge difference between growing a business from say $500,000 to $1 million, versus $5 million to $100 million. Those are two entirely different ventures and require a different perspective. A lot of times, the larger the gap between the start point and the desired endpoint, the more changes in perspective you will need to have along the way."

For all the sweat equity Jeff put into building his client base and growing the company, the transition from start-up entrepreneur to big picture managing partner of a fast-growth company is still a work in progress. "My role is constantly evolving," he says. "There are a number of things on my plate now that I would love to delegate, but certain aspects of the business are not at that critical mass point where it makes sense cost-wise to do that just yet."

Jeff believes that in terms of technical skills, what sets Neumeister & Associates apart from the competition and will help the company reach that critical mass sooner than later, is their methodology. "We approach all projects and all clients with a forensic lens, and usually that lens is pointed toward litigation matters that command premium expert witnessing. When we do traditional work like bookkeeping and tax prep, I just look at things like: *What's wrong here? What could go wrong here? Is there a more efficient way for them to structure their entity?* That's a perspective most accountants are not going to provide because they don't have the experience or ability to provide it. That ability is why we often find errors and missed opportunities by others that solely provide tax and bookkeeping services. We are also able to offer CFO services given our broad range of experience in other areas, including mergers and acquisitions, tax planning, and analytics."

The other area Jeff says that sets his company apart from the pack is its unique culture, which is informed by tenacity. It's a trait that clearly comes from the top, as reflected by the armful of degrees he earned, the credentials he's accrued, and his adventuresome athletic accomplishments. In addition to climbing Mt. Kilimanjaro in Tanzania— which he did because he said it sounded fun—he's also run the 150-mile Marathon Des Sables race across the Sahara Desert, where the racers have to carry all their own gear and food throughout the event. Next up Jeff plans to participate in the Jungle Marathon through the Amazon Rainforest.

"I have participated in hundreds of distance events, including dozens of marathons and half marathons. After a while those events began to feel too comfortable, so I started doing more ultra-endurance running. Those kinds of self-inflicted struggles have helped me to understand just how capable people are and that everyone has more potential than they realize. Physical challenges also make the obstacles you face growing a company seem less scary since I know I can overcome them. It taught me that whatever we think we're limited to is false," Jeff says. "We're capable of so much more. If I have to work thirty-seven hours straight to deal with a couple of time-sensitive client matters without any sleep, without any formal meal breaks, whatever, then so be it. Whatever it takes, I will make it happen. Now, I'm not advocating that's a healthy way to pursue a professional career, but my point is we will go above and beyond what most won't, and that's something I have embedded in the culture of my firm without me asking a single one of my staff to do. I lead by example. If they have to do something on a weekend, they just do it. It's not expected of them, it's not demanded of them, but they see what I do, what needs to be done for the client, and they follow that lead. They respect it, and they see what it can accomplish for our clients by doing so."

Whether an outgrowth of Jeff's single-mindedness and tenacity or the cause of it, long-distance running has been a way of life for years and will remain a core part of who he is. But he admits that the combined demands of work and having a young daughter mean carving out some me-time takes some juggling—something every entrepreneur must learn.

"It's an ongoing challenge that's being remedied in a gradual manner," Jeff says. "It wasn't uncommon for me to go into the office six or seven days a week. But my wife and I just closed on our house last week, and I'll actually have a legitimate home office. So between bringing my physical workspace home, having an able-bodied staff who know their roles now, and bringing a partner into the firm, I'll be able to cut that down to four or five days a week. I'm so proud to have tremendous team members with a great work ethic and who truly care about our clients. They have helped facilitate the growth of the firm."

Most of Jeff's staff are former students he'd met during his academic career, which started in 2012 as an adjunct at Westwood College in Los Angeles and has become a way for Jeff to mentor the next generation of industry leaders. "Helping to be that facilitator in someone's professional growth in understanding concepts is inherently rewarding. Teaching is also an extension of my current career path. There are definitely synergies involved in the business. For example, in the graduate classes I teach, I joke at the beginning of the course: *Don't think this is an accelerated seven-week course, think of this as a seven-week long interview,"* Jeff laughs. "And in some ways, it's true. Aside from all that, right now it's a side gig, but when I take a more passive role in the firm, teaching will probably become more of a full-time venture after I retire."

When peering into the future twenty, thirty years, Jeff envisions that passive role as being a kind of chairman emeritus, where he'd come into the office for maybe ten hours a week instead of seventy or eighty hours. "I'd interact with a few large, long-time clients, answer some questions, speak to the staff here and there, and that'll be the extent of my involvement."

Well, maybe he'll also spend some time mentoring and sharing hard-earned wisdom with up and coming entrepreneurs. "I think regardless of industry, you need to have a willingness to accept the challenge—and there will be challenges. And when things get difficult, you may feel like giving up at times but don't because those are indicators that you're probably on the right path. There were days starting this company where I'd wonder: *Why am I doing this?* There was a time when my accounts receivable balance was so low, I couldn't pay my employees. I couldn't pay rent minus our overhead time. That was extremely stressful, but you just have to work with it and through it."

Jeff often tells his students that today's successful professionals must never stop learning, inquiring, and devising innovative solutions to distinguish themselves. He says the key is seeing a problem in its full context.

"I consistently engage in research because every client is different from the other, and research provides an opportunity to investigate an industry, profile a company, and distill innovative strategies for addressing unique problems. There are a lot of CPAs who can easily replicate one another's work, but there are far fewer professionals who can tackle more unique or and complex problems."

In the end, it all comes back to tenacity. "Challenge yourself to get outside your comfort zones and meet the obstacle head-on," Jeff says. "As both a professor and as an entrepreneur, the people I've seen be the most successful are those who combine a willingness to accept daunting challenges, a commitment to do the advance work that positions you to have a competitive edge , and the belief that you can overcome any obstacle. As long as you have a strong work ethic, you can achieve anything."

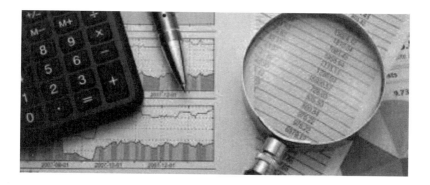

The point of taking vitamins and other supplements is to improve our health and wellness. But vitamin manufacturers add a variety of fillers and binders to their products that can include artificial sweeteners, alcohol, pork-based ingredients, shellfish, and hydrogenated oils—not exactly a menu in keeping with a my-body-is-a-temple credo.

Additives can pose a few different issues. Some consumers worry about potential allergic reactions, others prefer to avoid ingesting unnecessary chemicals or preservatives in vitamins on principle, and then there are those who need vitamins that adhere to their faith-based dietary restrictions such as Judaism's Kosher Law and Islam's halal. Perhaps the best-known example is pork, which is neither Kosher nor halal.

The number of Muslims in the United States is relatively small, comprising about 1.1 percent of the total population, so perhaps that's why the large supplement companies never spent the resources to target that niche market by developing vitamins that passed halal muster. Or perhaps it was more a decision colored by current political polarization. Either way, their loss was Noor Vitamins' gain.

When it launched in 2010, the New York-based company basically invented the halal supplements category in the United States, says one of the founders, Mohamed Issa. "Before us, there was no available choice for halal vitamins. We always had patients coming to us asking for medications, vitamins, and supplements that didn't contain non-halal products. But we never had a reputable, trusted brand that we could confidently recommend to them. A lot of big brands wouldn't go there, and that provided an opportunity for a smaller, more nimble company to fill the need. So we started Noor Vitamins to fill the void."

Noor Vitamins owns about 90 percent of the United States halal-certified market for supplements; worldwide they own about 75 percent. But Mohamed says he and his partners initially encountered a lot of naysayers.

"Many people laughed at us for coining the term *halal vitamins* as it was nonexistent, but now here we are today."

Noor Vitamins are made with scientifically formulated ingredients derived only from natural sources, and the company has no third-party contracts. Several of the formulations are patented and trademarked. More than just providing a quality product, Mohamed says it's equally important to educate consumers so they can ask the right questions.

"First, where are the ingredients from? Most vitamins contain a pork source because it's the most readily available and cheapest. What's the exact formula? You have to be careful with the daily dosage, so each supplement is scientifically formulated to have the correct dosage—no more, no less. What is FDA certification? Although the FDA doesn't certify vitamins or most manufacturers, our vitamins are produced in facilities that are FDA registered and Good Manufacturing Practices certified."

Noor's manufacturing facility and products are also certified halal, which ensures that any animals used within the process are treated in a humane fashion under Islamic principles. But Noor products are not simply halal; all the company's products are 100 percent natural. They're made with no artificial colors or preservatives, are non-GMO (genetically modified organisms), and gluten-free.

"Our mantra for the past couple of years has been to expand the value

Mohamed Issa

of our products beyond just being halal," Mohamed says. "We focus on producing a product that will be attractive to all consumers. Our growth is stemming mostly from the non-halal sector, and we believe that's the result of producing the highest-quality products we can—for everyone."

Noor wasn't Mohamed's first entrepreneurial rodeo. Over the course of his medical career, he has built, acquired, and managed several health care businesses. There's a reason that in addition to earning a pharmacology degree, he also has a degree in business administration as well. But Mohamed says his expertise in business was more circumstantial and serendipitous than a personal, professional agenda.

Born in Egypt, Mohamed and his family moved to the United States when he was a young boy. They lived modestly in Queens, New York, as they established roots in their new country. Eventually Mohamed started picking up various jobs in the neighborhood to contribute to the family's finances.

"Unlike other positions where you would punch a clock and get paid the seven dollars an hour, sales and marketing jobs were performance-based," he explains. "The more you sold, or the more you marketed, the better you made out, so out of necessity, those were the positions I went for."

That held true as he worked his way through college and while earning his doctorate in pharmacology. "Again, working in a hospital or in a pharmacy would not have enabled me to help my family the way I needed to as well as help pay for my education and all the things that come with those responsibilities."

By the time he'd earned his pharmacology degree, Mohamed had about a decade of sales and marketing experience. As he reflected on his potential career options, it occurred to Mohamed he could make the biggest health care impact by combining his business experience and medicine.

"That's where the juncture came together," he says. "It wasn't something I contemplated while I was studying medicine; it just happened in retrospect after I got my degree."

As part of his post-doctoral fellowship program, Mohamed was required to work in different aspects of medicine, including as a clinical pharmacist. He says he was emotionally drawn to the clinical setting because he was able to help one patient at a time.

"That was great. And I could have certainly found fulfillment in that. Many people do."

But Mohamed had a sense of urgency to help as many people as he could, so his focus was to impact populations as opposed to individuals. "It's the merger of health care and medicine, business decisions, research and development strategies, and products you can make available that can transform how populations of people are being cared for in the health care space. That's what drove me to the business side of healthcare. I could make an impact in a shorter timeframe versus seeing one patient at a time. Again, that approach has great value, and I applaud anyone who does it that way. I just was drawn to a different type of impact-making."

In utilizing his business experience and medical training, Mohamed has managed companies for others, founded start-ups, and acquired established businesses. But over time he came to define his professional purpose, which is to save and sustain human life through health care innovation. That vision is what now directs and defines his career path.

"After years of reflecting, gaining different experiences, and thinking about what it was I wanted to leave behind in this world, that's it," he says. "And in any health care business or dynamic, that is my driving force. So today I just chase that purpose. Now clearly, when leading larger organizations there's always an affinity toward setting a clear vision, setting clear objectives, having metrics that are easily understood and measured to assess your progress against that purpose. But I believe all that means nothing if you don't anchor vision into a clear purpose to galvanize broader groups of people behind something that really matters, something way bigger than themselves—that's purpose."

Vision, impact, and purpose came together with the creation of Noor Pharmaceuticals, which began as an idea to help the local Muslim community when a pharmacist friend who was practicing in the community approached Mohamed and suggested they start a combination medical clinic-pharmacy. They got together with two other colleagues, one of which was Mohamed's sister, who is a pharmacist as well. When brainstorming about how to make the proposed business different from established pharmacies like Walgreens or CVS, the lack of halal supplements came up.

"The idea came up to create a clinic that was very local in nature, to make a difference there. But then once we started looking into vitamins and supplements, we realized that whenever we were making recommendations for vitamins and supplements to patients who have more dietary restrictions—whether it be halal, Kosher, or vegan—there weren't any suitable brand that they felt comfortable recommending. The problem of finding any that didn't contain pork or alcohol or shellfish was not just a local problem; it was a global problem. I was taken aback by that, and suddenly the opportunity seemed much bigger than a local one."

It should be noted that in Islam, supplements are not looked at the same way as medicines. A cancer medication with pork or alcohol as an ingredient would be permissible because it was prescribed as a matter of life and death. But vitamins and supplements are voluntary, which makes those ingredients non-permissible.

Mohamed says after they searched and failed to find alternatives they could offer patients, he suggested they provide the product. "I relied on my experience in the pharmaceutical world and said: *Hey, why don't we just create it? Why don't we just build it?* So we put together a business plan and pitched for the resources required to start the venture."

Like a lot of start-ups, Mohamed and his partners had to make their idea work with fewer resources than they would have liked. "We were fortunate to have investors and funding for the company, but it was exponentially less than what we would have had in my corporate setting, for example."

Mohamed notes their experience is a teaching moment for up and coming entrepreneurs. "Consider what you think you need to start a business and then cut it by about ten times," he advises. "That's what you'll likely have, so make it work. Whenever you think you can't, you usually can, so just go get it done."

Despite having a steadfast belief in their idea, Mohamed admits that there were moments when he wondered if it would all come together. "Any entrepreneur that tells you that they don't at some point doubt themselves, doubt the concept, doubt their stamina, doubt whether or not it's worth it, would be lying," he says with a laugh. "Entrepreneurship is literally an emotional roller coaster. One day you think you're the on top of the world, and the next day you just don't know how you're going to make it. Summoning the stamina required to

In respoonse to COVID-19, Noor developed a suppllement to boost the immune system.

make it through that roller coaster, while being emotionally aware and poised, usually determines whether people are successful and not."

Noor's do or die moment for Mohamed came when they launched the brand at a consumer trade show. That same weekend the company website was going online, and the marketing campaign was going live.

"We had people in the back office turning the website on while my co-founders and I were packing one thousand boxes of vitamins into the back of a van," he recalls.

As the leader of the group, Mohamed had his game face on, exuding confidence they were going to crush it at the convention by selling all their products and generating momentum-building launch buzz. But during the seven-hour drive to the trade show—flying was cost prohibitive—Mohamed says while his mouth was saying: *Of course we're going to do great,* his heart and brain were fretting. *Oh, man, I hope we do great. What will we do if we don't sell one box?*

"I was dreading the thought of having to pack all those boxes back into the van and drive home with them. But I couldn't show that doubt because I was leading the group. If I showed doubt, then they would doubt, and it would just be a spiral effect from there."

His outward confidence was rewarded. Before they had finished setting up their booth, the Noor team had sold about fifty bottles by word of mouth. "Other exhibitors and vendors were coming up saying: *I want to grab one of my own before you sell out.* We drove back with an empty van, and that's when I thought: *We're onto something.*"

It's also when Noor's investors became more excited that they had caught supplement lightning in a bottle. That led to Noor receiving more resources, and that helped the company evolve its value proposition from the "halal Centrum" positioning to establishing a formidable supplement brand in the mainstream market space.

Noor Vitamins launched in 2010 with four products—a multivitamin, a prenatal, a calcium-vitamin D, and a children's vitamin—marketed as an alternative to Centrum that just happened to be halal-based. Since then company's offerings have expanded to include patented proprietary formulas produced in-house.

"Because the formula—organic, all-natural, vegan products—is our trademark, the value proposition is no longer: *We're as good as them, just halal.* Now it's: *We are the most comprehensive vitamin supplement on the market that happens to be halal,*" Mohamed says. "Our formulas are scientifically-backed, and we source our ingredients from the best possible natural sources. We also have independent lab testing to confirm purity and potency and offer the broadest line of vitamins in the category. So we've been fortunate to go from just a halal-alternative to what we believe is a best-in-class vitamin and supplement brand that we give our own families."

The ingredients other manufacturers use, such as pork and shellfish, do serve a purpose, whether as a binding agent or to stabilize the compounds. So replacing those typical ingredients to create an all-natural supplement took a lot of time, effort, and cost.

"It was certainly a difficult process," Mohamed admits. "But when building any start-up, things will always be hard. You just can't be deterred by that difficulty; you have to work through it. And one way to do that is by surrounding yourself with smart people who know more than you. We were able to recruit behind our vision, a group of pharmacologists who are absolutely stellar at what they do, and they were able to identify scientific alternatives to those ingredients. All that started with my co-founders; without them we'd literally not exist."

Since its first line of products in 2010, Noor has continued to look for new offerings, such as protein powder, gummies, and a fish oil supplement, which is sourced from Peruvian cold-water fisheries. Mohamed says the process for identifying what products they want to market next is based on data that indicates what products are most needed by consumers.

"Then the next question in our algorithm is, which of those products have non-permissible ingredients or which of those products can we scientifically improve through better ingredients or formulas? From there we prioritize the products that we launch based on the market uptake. By using that process the right way, we typically find ourselves with more products to make than we usually have the capacity to do. So we have a pipeline of products we are always actively developing. That's why we have the broadest product line for the whole family. We don't just have gummies. We don't just have tablets. We don't just have softgels. We don't just have things for men or women or children or the elderly. We don't just have specialty products like joint and energy supplements, we have the entire portfolio."

While Noor may not have had any competition when they started, they do now—sort of. "Every two years or so there will be a competitor that launches, and then they'll go away," he says. "But seriously, we welcome that. We find that when competitors launch, they actually grow the market because they reach consumers that we might not have. We also find that when market education takes place and consumers go through their due diligence on the products and the brands that have the most credibility, most history, most complete formulas, most competent manufacturing, and the most naturally-sourced ingredients, we're very confident that they'll make the right selection: Noor. Not to mention, competition keeps us on our toes to constantly get better. So competition is a great thing."

Another aspect that differentiates Noor is having its own FDA-certified facilities, where other supplements brands contract manufacturing. "That model is fundamentally different because you're not controlling your own supply chain," Mohamed explains. "Also, we test the potency of our products through independent labs as part of their certification, making sure that what's on our label is actually in the product. I can tell you even the major brands don't do that."

KEEPING YOUR ENTIRE FAMILY HEALTHY FOR OVER 10 YEARS
Find the right vitamins for you!

The upshot is the ingredient list for vitamins may not always be completely accurate—something not controlled by regulators. Mohamed estimates that many supplement products sold don't contain what the packaging says they do. Despite the red tape it would create, the Noor founders have become vocal advocates for more regulations in the supplement space because they believe having authorities with expertise oversee products will make them safer.

The last piece of Noor's value proposition is a commitment to social causes and giving back to the community. To that end about 3 percent of net earnings go to charitable donations, made either through products or direct financial support which is in line with Islamic business practices and giving charitable donations.

"We feel strongly about making a social impact," Mohamed says. "It's not just making the best possible product, it's not just giving customers the best possible experience, but it's also leaving your community better than you received it. And I think if we do those three things well, we will naturally find success."

An issue almost every company faces now is the threat of counterfeits, where fake product brands are passed off as the real thing. Counterfeiting of medicines is a growing problem around the world. It's one thing to accidentally buy a fake Kate Spade purse, quite another something you ingest because counterfeit medicines are generally made from lower quality components and can be harmful or even fatal to patients. In addition to pursuing copycats to the fullest extent of current law, Mohamed tries to minimize the public's exposure to counterfeit products.

"For us it's less about them copying us and more about educating our consumers about where and how to get our products," he says. "When consumers don't have access to a product, they look for different venues to have access. Access is also based on price; if the price is too high, consumers will look for an alternative. We've successfully built a credible network of outlets where consumers can buy our products at an affordable price point, even with all the cost incurred to make a best-in-class portfolio. They can buy from us directly. They can buy from Amazon, we're in about a thousand pharmacies here in the States. Our products are found internationally through authorized resellers. So if you can make the best products available, if you can create effective and efficient access for consumers, and if you can educate them directly on how to make those choices, I think those copycats go away pretty quickly."

As Noor Vitamins has grown, the division of labor among the founders has evolved and differentiated. Mohamed admits he's a bit OCD when it comes to clarity of vision, clarity of strategy, and clarity of roles and responsibilities. While today his role has evolved to board management, general management oversight, periodically dealing with investors, and helping the day-to-day team set the broader strategy for the company, he notes that in any start-up environment, founders don't yet have the luxury of clearly defining categorical rules and responsibilities because so much needs to get done.

"You simply don't have enough hands on deck," he says. "So my partners and I were just amazingly collaborative. Without my partners this company wouldn't be here today."

Those partners come from a variety of healthcare backgrounds. Dina Khairie is a pharmacist, the company's head of medical strategy and communication, and supports in product formulation and development. In the early days she oversaw marketing campaigns on Noor's website and social media. Dina is also Mohamed's sister and he says she's the "better version of him in every way personally and professionally."

Hamza Malik is Noor's chief science officer, who leads vitamin research and new product development teams. He supervises the company's manufacturing facilities and oversees product production, including raw material analysis, quality assurance, and regulatory compliance.

Mohamed says, "It was actually Hamza's idea to start this business. He's more visionary than his humble nature lets on."

Majid Bukhari is an engineer oversees all Noor operations, including regulatory compliance and execution of international initiatives. According to Mohamed Majid is the "heart and soul of Noor."

Mohamed also gives a nod to Salahu Din Kwo, Kazi Islam, and Mohamed Salama, early team members who helped start Noor that are no longer with the company. "Everyone brings a bit of a different lens to the conversation in different expertise. But we also were very quick to help each other out, especially in the earlier phases of the venture when everyone is doing everything. It didn't matter what needed to be done; if someone needed a hand, we would just help them. Then as your company grows and as you're able to make it more sustainable, those divisions of labor become clearer. Those leaders either move on to other roles externally, which is great for them, or stay at Noor and hire people underneath them who can help carry the load, and people naturally start to fall into areas of their respective expertise."

Mohamed says one of the best pieces of advice he could give a would-be entrepreneur is that to build a sustainable business, you have to work with and hire the best people that you blindly trust. "First and foremost they must have character as well as the work ethic, passion, grit, and selflessness required to start any venture. They must also have an aptitude, an expertise in their respective fields. I've had the best of both worlds—the best of character and the best of aptitude—with the partners I was fortunate enough to start Noor Vitamins with."

He also believes another factor in both his ability to comfortably ease into the CEO role and the company's success was his experience working in pharma Corporate America. "The structure, operational savvy, and leadership required to be successful in that environment made me better at Noor because I brought a certain level of structure, operations, long-term strategy, long-term vision development, and people leadership, which is what I was doing in my day job, and then the entrepreneurship and the grit and the hustle at Noor made me better in the big corporate environment. So I think having a foot in both for some time made that transition easier and also more effective."

There was another advantage of not quitting his salaried job until Noor was on more solid footing. While a lot of entrepreneurs believe you must quit everything and be all in on your start-up, Mohamed doesn't subscribe to that. Keeping his day job meant he didn't have to think about personal financial considerations in guiding Noor, which helped him make better long-term decisions. Mohamed says he was already accustomed to working more than one hundred hours a week from his early upbringing, calling it second nature.

"Because my bills were covered through my day job, I wasn't desperate to make a sale, nor was I desperate to sign the wrong deal. I said no to Walmart, and people said I was absolutely crazy. But had I signed with Walmart our second year in business, we would have gone out of business because the amount of resources needed to make products to stock their shelves, and their payment cycles, and the margins they push to be competitive, we could not have sustained that. We would have an amazing two years but would have failed in the long term. And to be honest, if I weren't working in my day job, I would have signed Walmart because I would have been desperate to make that work."

Having outside income also enabled Mohamed to reinvest 100 percent of the proceeds back into Noor. "We weren't extracting any profit from the company for a long time, so we were comfortable operating at break even or a little bit in the negative because we knew we'd be okay."

Looking at how far Noor has come, Mohamed says he's proud of what they've been able to accomplish. Looking forward, he sees continued growth for Noor and more entrepreneurial ventures for himself.

"Any entrepreneur who doesn't have some sort of exit strategy is not telling you the truth," he says. "But it's not just about a financial exit. If my purpose is to save and sustain human life through health care innovation, then an exit makes the most sense because at some point Noor in someone else's hands may make it more scalable than in my hands. If I'm doing this for the right reason setting Noor up to reach and help more people should be just as attractive as a buyout for the founders. Right now we're in thirteen countries. I'm sure there is a company out there that can get Noor products into one hundred or more countries. So giving more people access while also creating an opportunity for us to start our next venture is a mutually beneficial exit I can happily live with."

NoorVitamins
Combining Simplicity & Unmatched Purity

✳ Oxygen Orchard

It's basic Biology 101; oxygen is essential to human life. There's an old medical rule of thumb that estimates humans can survive three weeks without food and three days without water, but only about three minutes without oxygen. Your body's cells need oxygen for cellular respiration, the process that enables cells to convert fuel into life-sustaining energy. Try holding your breath for more than a minute, and oxygen's importance becomes uncomfortably clear.

Likewise, our bodies need water for proper cell, muscle, and brain function. Since water is comprised of molecules of oxygen and hydrogen (H_2O), it seems logical that oxygenating water would offer health benefits beyond hydration. That idea is behind Oxygen Orchard's The Big Pitcher, which infuses oxygen into your drinking water in a matter of minutes. But what founder Teri Mathis based the company on was science.

"It is a medical fact that our bodies need oxygen for healthy living," she says. "Because of lifestyle choices, our cells may demand more oxygen than our pulmonary systems can deliver. The Big Pitcher is a convenient and safe way to supplement your body's oxygen. Your drinking water should have the highest possible natural saturation of oxygen, which is about eleven parts per million. We have designed a durable, attractive appliance to add the maximum safe amount of oxygen to your drinking water."

Teri stresses that this is not a glorified water filter. "Filtering is *so* twentieth century," she laughs. "We're all about oxygen."

The seeds for The Big Pitcher were sown in early 2000 when she measured her family's drinking water to see how much dissolved oxygen it contained. It wasn't as out of left field as it might sound because water was Teri's business.

After spending many years working at brokerages, including Merrill Lynch and PaineWebber, she went to work for a venture capital company, where she met a chemist. "He was just starting an environmental remediation business. This was in the mid-'80s when everybody and their dog were starting small businesses to clean up petroleum, hydrocarbon waste, spills, and other environmental things like that," Teri says. "I worked for him for several years—cheap to free—because I was fascinated with the organic chemistry part of it. When I started my company, Bio-Tex Environmental, in the late 1980s, he was fine with that because I was treating industrial wastewater—with my steel-toed boots and hardhat—generated by chemical and plastic plants to meet certain state and federal requirements, while his business was in treating contaminated soils."

Teri was more than an administrator and field worker; she was also an innovator. "I realized I needed to provide my clients with a less expensive device to aerate the ponds I was treating. They had been using what was called a *donut* that oxygenated the water by pushing it up in the air in a circular shape and required a lot of power. The aerator I developed used less than half the electricity as the donuts. I installed them in several facilities, and it worked beautifully. It was much less expensive for the client and provided a larger influence of oxygen."

One of the instruments she used, called YSI 55, was a meter that measured dissolved oxygen. "The higher the level of oxygen, the cleaner the water is. Typically in those ponds and lagoons, the oxygen level was extremely low. So I would design our treatment protocol accordingly. Out of curiosity one day at home, I measured our drinking water, which came

Teri Mathis

from a well. There was zero dissolved oxygen because there was no air-water interface between the well and our faucet."

That same day Teri started searching for a product she could buy that would oxygenate her family's drinking water. There was nothing in stores or online.

Teri notes that there also wasn't much centralized information available about the effects of drinking water with little to no dissolved oxygen. "This was around 2000, and the Internet then wasn't what it is now, but there wasn't anything in the marketplace that we could find," she says. "So over the next three years, my husband and I did a ton of research and development."

The more she learned, the more she believed her idea had legs. Eventually she began work on developing a product that would infuse oxygen into their drinking water.

"It was a lot of trial and error. Some of the prototypes were comical because they just were just so bad," she admits with a laugh. "But like I tell people, you can't be afraid to make mistakes. We certainly did although none that would cost us our business. And we finally developed a system we felt pretty confident about, and that's how I got into the healthy appliance business."

Teri and her husband started selling their units in 2005. But they faced an ongoing obstacle that is familiar to many American entrepreneurs: the difficulty of finding home-grown manufacturing. "We really tried to get most of our parts in America, but if it's not made here, you have to get it somewhere else. So much of the manufacturing had been sent overseas, and that was a real challenge from the start."

Not just logistically but quality control as well. Teri recalls how in 2016, they started getting calls from customers saying their pitcher was cracking. They honored the warranty and replaced the defective pitchers—for the next three years.

"We had gotten a bad batch from overseas. Plastic injection is very complex. We don't know what exactly, but they did something wrong. So in the spring of 2018, we made the tough decision to bring our custom parts molds from overseas, close to three tons of carbon steel."

Teri notes the decision was not without risk. "For one thing, we didn't know if US plastic injection companies could utilize those molds, meaning we weren't sure that we could even have the parts made. Plus, shipping is very expensive, so it cost us a lot of money to bring the molds over. And I had to pay the new tariff that had just gone into effect. I spent many hours on the phone with the US Customs folks. And during all that we were also taking care of our existing customer base, keeping them close and happy. Somehow we did that for three years. It was a miracle."

Teri says the August day they arrived at the Port of Houston "was a happy day for us. And thankfully, we were able to use our molds, so the risk paid off. We also made a change in the high-end plastic we used for the pitchers. We decided to use a compound called Triton made by Eastman Materials in Franklin, Tennessee, for the pitcher. We had been introduced to Triton at a trade show a few years prior. We liked the company a lot, and we loved that Triton was BPA-free, perfectly food grade, and literally unbreakable."

For as difficult it had been researching and designing the product, marketing The Big Pitcher was a whole other matter. In addition to the nuts and bolts of developing prototypes, applying for their patent, and figuring out how to become a manufacturer, there was also the matter of exposure and—especially—education.

Teri says the value of oxygen-infused water comes down to basic cellular biology. "Cells have various functions such as maintaining immunity, performing their designed function such as brain, skin, or pancreas detoxifying, and reproducing."

FOOD + OXYGEN = ENERGY.
A simple key to weight reduction is to try to introduce the right foods to your body but remember that the oxygen part of the equation is just as important.

Oxygen Orchard

But it could be argued one of the most important is managing the conversion of nutrients to energy. "Think of it as the formula nutrients (food) + oxygen = energy. The quality of the energy that a cell has to produce is dependent on the nutrients and the oxygen. The world is obsessed with the diet part, the nutrients. What we've done is to introduce oxygen to the marketplace. If you don't have enough oxygen, you're going to have health problems. It's as simple as that."

Teri says when they first started out, "The public had never really thought: *I need to be drinking oxygen-infused water,* much less *I need to supplement my body's oxygen levels,* however much that might be. We had to overcome that. What we did was real innovation. Nobody else knew what I knew about the physics of water and oxygen or of what drinking oxygen-infused water could do. Not many people knew about bioremediation[1] using microbes and oxygen."

The specialization of knowledge that was behind The Big Pitcher technology also made hiring sales associates problematic. "I didn't want to try to convince them, number one, or number two train them in all I knew. And that was in the beginning; now there's much more research, so bringing people up-to-speed who work with us—as well as those who

---

[1] The use of either naturally occurring or deliberately introduced microorganisms or other forms of life to consume and break down environmental pollutants, in order to clean up a polluted site.

want to work with us—is still one of my main challenges. It's not easy because most of the population is all about supplements, vitamins, green smoothies, and diet, diet, diet when improving your oxygen balance is equally as important—if not more important—to create the energy your cells need. Most people think that if you're breathing, you have all the oxygen you need."

One of the potential dangers of not having enough oxygen is a weakening of the immune system. After COVID-19 spread all around the world, Teri says consumers started their own research on how to strengthen their immune systems in light of a global pandemic, and she saw a significant uptick in sales since the virus hit our shores.

"I have so much respect and admiration for American consumers because they got it. All of a sudden people were talking about oxygen levels in their bodies, and it just coincided with the day we re-opened the doors for business. And boom, we started getting purchase orders. But beyond the virus, The Big Pitcher is for everybody, even if you're not immuno-compromised. Let's face it; we have to deal with a great deal of stress in this world we live in, we deal with air pollution, we deal with foods that aren't pure. And everything we ingest, whether it's drinks, alcoholic beverages, prescription medications, or vitamins, it all has to be metabolized. And that takes oxygen."

How The Big Pitcher works is straightforward. The technology uses diffusion.

"There are only four ways to infuse water with oxygen," Teri says. "The way we do it is by pulling in ambient air—in other words the air that we're breathing. The O_2 dissolves or transfers into the water as those bubbles rise slowly through the column of water in The Big Pitcher. And as that's happening, your water oxygen level is getting higher, up to 95 or 96 percent. Our lab tested some of our water at 98 percent."

---

[2] The oxygen we breathe are molecules of two oxygen atoms combined, hence O_2.

The reason the oxygen doesn't dissipate into the air around us when the water is poured into a glass is a matter of physics, Teri says. "It's not under pressure. Here's the example I like to give. Consider two bodies of water. One is a small ditch full of decaying leaves under the hot summer sun. You will find very little oxygen in that water, compared to the air-borne droplets at, say, Niagara Falls, which is super-saturated with oxygen because of the water-oxygen interface. The oxygenation in The Big Pitcher is all natural. And there's no such thing as oxygen toxicity, so you can't drink too much of it. That's the difference between ours and alkaline water."

Teri says the diffuser, also called the air chamber, of the pitcher lasts four to six months, often longer, before needing replacement. "We have just the one replaceable part, so the pitcher and base and everything inside the base should theoretically last indefinitely."

While Teri developed the technology based on her extensive research and experience—which she used to author *Full Circle: The Role of Oxygen in Health*—she is careful to avoid the exaggerations other health products make. The claims she makes have been well-researched, and every statement in her marketing can be backed up with scientific fact. Teri feels validated in her belief that drinking oxygen-infused water promotes wellness by fifteen years of customer's testimonials, supported by her original research.

"John Duncan, a research scientist at Texas Women's University, did a double-blind study in 1998 where he divided amateur athletes into two groups. He gave one group bottled oxygen-infused water and the other group regular bottled water. Then he had them run a 5K. He reported that 83 percent of those drinking the oxygen-infused water posted a personal best time. I went to Denton, Texas, to meet with him, and he was very generous and gracious. In his opinion the results were statistically significant. The problem is that very little testing has been done in the field. But that's changing. In a recent study, sick rats were given oxygen-infused water to drink, and across the board the rats got better."

But other research seems to be bringing oxygen's role in the body to the fore, such as the 2019 Nobel Prize for Physiology or Medicine going to three scientists studying how cells adapt to oxygen availability.

"They were doing research on hypoxia, which describes cells not having enough oxygen," Teri says. "Honestly, this research wasn't happening ten years ago, studies showing that yes, hypoxia can cause cancers, diabetes, and obesity. Of course I already knew that," she says with a laugh. "But good. Let them come along and help me prove it. Let them find some money to do clinical testing. We have even established our own research company for that very reason. Discovering the truth about the role of oxygen, that's what I really want because our business is in an enviable position when all that starts to happen."

To make sure they are optimally positioned, Teri is looking to continue improving manufacturing efficiencies and keep developing marketing strategies. "I'm a marketing person. In my first career I was a registered securities broker for fifteen years. That's the ultimate sales position. So frankly I thought marketing our product would be easier and was a little surprised when it wasn't. For example, I love trade shows, but regretfully trade shows don't work very well for us. It always costs us more

to go to one than we recoup. We don't come out with a profit because our product is not an impulse buy. But those shows are where I do my on-the-ground market research, and I love talking to people about our amazing product. And we're able to educate a lot of people and be educated by them."

Instead she has built a stable of resellers, including retailers such as Walmart.com. and b8ta stores, a little mom-and-pop in Colorado that sells The Big Pitcher to help offset the low oxygen problems they have at higher altitudes, and a catalog that is distributed all over the country. "Our years in business have certainly helped, and now, resellers are contacting me—the best low-effort, high-reward marketing of all. And we're expanding to Canada and Europe within the next twelve months."

Teri feels especially fortunate that her previous two careers helped shape her for this one. She admits that part of being an entrepreneur can be a slog and requires a lot of patience and determination.

"You reach out, you send a sample, you write letters and make phone calls and hope someone calls you back. But often they don't. So there are a lot of prayers. But look, I was the kid who went door to door selling flower seeds to earn an ant farm. It's something that's been in my blood my entire life. It's just who I am."

Teri says her targets are wide-ranging, including pitching her product to medical device companies that specialize in helping people living with COPD and emphysema as well as water delivery companies like Culligan.

"This is what I love about my business. You might run into a brick wall over here, like no response from a Walgreens for instance—which, by the way, look at their product line every other year, so nothing happens fast in this business. But if that door closes, there are so many others to go through. The landscape changes daily; it's just infinitely challenging and fun because who knows what's going to work next. And when it does, we know that it's going to be huge."

The high-risk, high-reward aspect of being an entrepreneur isn't for the faint of heart, but Teri says she's never really had a guaranteed paycheck throughout her professional life. "I've never had a salary job. I was a stockbroker, and that was commission only. When I started my environmental company, that wasn't a guaranteed paycheck for sure. But when I got one, it was pretty big. This is my third career, so it's what I'm used to."

She's also never let the challenge of introducing a novel product get in her way. "It's not hard, and here's why. When I first started I went from being a sales assistant at Merrill Lynch to getting my broker's license, which was not an easy thing. I had no sales experience, but I never had a doubt. I am over-endowed with ambition," she laughs. "Now, it might be blind and really stupid ambition, but it comes in handy when you want to start a company. And I never had a doubt because I did my early research to answer the question: *Does this make any sense at all?* And listen; it's not just going to happen like little fairy dust coming down. You have to make your mind up to make it happen."

With this product especially, Teri feels like she is improving lives while also developing lifelong friendships with some of her customers. "My husband and I love to help people, and that's what we get to do every day."

Teri also spends time sharing her entrepreneurial knowledge and experience with the next generation of innovators.

"Sam Houston State University is a really well-respected college in Texas, and they offer a bachelor of business administration in entrepreneurship. Every year I get invited there to speak to the seniors."

The life experience she offers is far-ranging. "I tell them, you know, masters have failed more than beginners have tried. Pick the right significant other or spouse who will support you. You can't do it if you've got somebody next to you who's taking away your self-esteem or your ambition. It's a creative process as much as creating a piece of art is, requiring imagination, self-discipline, and courage. But that's where you get to really have fun. So many people don't have fun. But man, if you do it right and you're doing what you want to do, it's fun. I'm one of those lucky few who has enjoyed all three of my careers. I've enjoyed every single minute of working, and I feel so blessed because it's been exactly what I've wanted to do."

She also tells the students to persist. "If you believe, never give up. Sure, you can give up if it's something that's not going to work and shows itself to be utterly impossible beyond the shadow of a doubt. Even then it doesn't necessarily mean you throw the baby out with the bathwater. Try pivoting."

For as much as she enjoys her work, Teri acknowledges the clock is ticking for her time at Oxygen Orchard. "I'm going to retire when I'm seventy-five years old, which is in 2023. And honestly, I don't think I'm the one who can grow the company as big as I think it can be with the capital it will need. SodaStream is another company that uses gas diffusion into beverages. Pepsi just bought them for $3.2 billion. So I'm going to work really hard in the next few years and then sell. That's going to be the happiest/saddest day for me."

While Teri says she'll be happy to consult for a year or two, getting the new owners up to speed with the technology and the science, she has other plans she's eager to devote her time to.

"But my next project after selling is to continue researching, writing, and speaking about oxygen. There's a lot of misunderstanding about oxygen. It's the gas that gets no respect. People need to learn, and they need to be aware of their body's oxygen balance. That's where the rubber meets the road and is the difference between health and disease."

The world has always been a dangerous place, for some much more than others. History taught us early on that the more powerful, successful, or despotic someone was, the more they needed to watch their back. In 1,300 BC Egyptian Pharaoh Ramses II privately hired Nubian, Syrian, and Libyan warriors to protect him and his possessions. A thousand years later in Greece, seven of Alexander the Great's closest friends were named his *somatophylakes*, or bodyguards, positions of both great honor and influence. Since then many societies throughout the world have utilized personal security forces for those in high places, such as the medieval knights in Great Britain, the Vatican's Swiss Guard, the Musketeers of the Guard for the king in seventeenth-century France, and today's Secret Service.

What connects bodyguards across millennia is an inherent willingness to put oneself in harm's way to protect others' life, property, or position. Whether driven by ideology, monetary gain, or personal relationships, security is a profession that requires courage, focus, and commitment. And for as much as civilization had advanced, the world remains a dangerous place and the demand for personal security continues to grow. According to industry reports, private security is expected to generate more than $39 billion in 2020.

Helping spur that growth is RiP USA, self-described on its website as a high-value, low-exposure private security and investigative organization. "We operate in multiple sectors protecting human life and valuable property. RiP USA is additionally a training group that focuses on building high-value professionals who are ready to meet the changing needs of various protective and operational contracts."

When founded by US Army sniper Duztin Watson in 2012, the company's goal was to use his expertise in surveillance, counter-terrorism, and small unit tactics to provide the best-trained and highest-quality private security force available in the United States. Today the company has grown into a nationwide presence headquartered in Pittsburgh, Pennsylvania. Much of RiP's executive team and employees are former veterans or first responders, and the company's name was designed in part to reflect their military influences and values:

Remembrance. *We live in the shadows of the past. We are only able to succeed because of the platform past generations have built for us. RiP is a living memorial to every man or woman that has benefited our future in any way. Be it through innovation and design or the giving of life on the battlefield. Historical achievements and hardship echo within the walls of RiP; our professional, courteous, and humble demeanor resonate our appreciation to be here serving you today.*

Innovation. *Our company will strive in every way to provide high-quality security professionals effectively meeting the needs of individuals or companies seeking protection, security, or training. We also provide top tier security consulting and risk management services. RiP has a unique experience portfolio allowing innovative and custom catered security and protection solutions.*

Progression. *We focus our energy on progression-based security solutions. We constantly seek to better our level of training, seek out and acquire updated or more efficient equipment, and increase our ability to work safely in whatever situation we find ourselves. We are constantly moving forward to better ourselves and our company.*

Duztin Watson

Duztin says the star over the I in the logo signifies *you are here.* "It's a visual reminder that you are only able to be right here, right now because of past innovators and progressive personalities. These amazing individuals cut their own path and followed their dreams. Here at RiP we never lose sight of or forget what others have sacrificed to allow us these modern opportunities. We thank every man and woman who has sacrificed to build all of us a better tomorrow."

From the time he was a kid, Duztin knew he was a protector by nature. "I've always been a physically fit, very powerful, very strong individual. I did mixed martial arts and jujutsu to hone my skills. If someone came at me, I'd eat a lot of crow. But if they were treating someone else poorly, I was quick to lash out to protect that person because I knew bullying was inherently wrong."

While security may seem like a natural segue from military service and for someone who was protective by nature, Duztin's professional path wasn't always a given, especially as a youth when he took some detours along the way. "My father was very rough and aggressive and had a significant criminal history. He was in and out of prison," he says. "My mother had been in some trouble as well. Early on I knew I didn't want to follow that path. That would not be the way to a productive life."

Even so, as Duztin points out it can be hard for the apple to propel itself away from the tree. Children are prone to pick up traits they see at home, and as an adolescent he did have some temper issues.

"But again, it was usually in relation to defending others. So from a very young age, all the aggression from living in a dysfunctional home was channeled through my heart and became my life's mission to serve and protect others. That's why I wanted to join the military and live a life of service."

But first he had to make it through high school, which was admittedly not a good fit for him. "Sitting down in a chair, working on a computer, building spreadsheets—that's not my strong suit. But taking apart intricate, elaborate technology and rebuilding it, that's always been great for me. I've always been good at understanding mechanics, learn quickly, and am good with my hands. I would help my father fix all our vehicles. And being from Houston my family was very blue-collar; they always had cars up on jacks," he says with a laugh. "But being raised poor, automobiles were super flashy to me. The coolest thing you could ever possibly strive to have was a cool car."

When he was eighteen Duztin tried his hand at starting his own metal fabrication business, where he repurposed, rebuilt, and reformed steel to create custom air ride suspension. "It was a fun experience, and I had some success," he says. "But I was an eighteen-year-old young man going into business thinking I knew it all at that age, so it ultimately did not work out for me. But it taught me some important lessons."

And not just about business. While running his business, a friend had a car they wanted to get rid of, and Duztin agreed to take it apart.

"It sounded exciting to have a vehicle to do whatever I wanted to. We tore the vehicle up and set it on fire, which got me arrested and indicted for felony arson. At the time I didn't understand there was this big legal system out there that could damage and destroy my life. I didn't understand how big of a deal the charge was even though nobody was hurt, just the car."

Soon enough he realized what the consequences could be, so facing the judge was a come to Jesus moment. Although the judge showed mercy, she also made it clear he needed an attitude adjustment. He was given an opportunity to prove himself as a productive member of society and make restitution. The charges were ultimately dismissed after satisfactorily completing the terms and guidelines set by the court.

"The judge said: *We're going to make this a lesser offense. We're going to make it something that you can live with. But the reason we have laws that say what is unacceptable is that a fireman responding to the fire could have been injured or killed because of your foolish behavior. This is not a game, young man.* She looked right into my soul, and I took every word in. It got me off the path of being a follower. I knew I needed to be a leader. I had to be responsible for my actions and my decisions. It was good the system was there to not only scare me straight but to also give me a second chance and recognize people make stupid mistakes. That was a huge pivot point in my life from where I could have ended up to where I am now."

While his felony charge didn't ruin his life, it would later complicate it, and Duztin would pay a heavy consequence for his moment of firebug thoughtlessness. "It did damage me. I missed out on many opportunities. When I joined the military, I was completely set on going to Ranger school, being attached to a Ranger battalion, and if that wasn't an option, then I was going to try and go ODA," which is the primary fighting force of the Green Berets.

While the Army Rangers are an elite light infantry unit tasked with missions like direct action raids, reconnaissance, and personnel recovery, the Green Berets are the Army's Special Forces whose role includes unconventional warfare. Operational Detachment Alpha (ODA) is the primary fighting force of the Green Berets. ODAs are made up of twelve men, each with a separate military occupational specialty.

"I was not eligible for any of that because of the arson incident," Duztin says. "So they waivered me into the military, and because I was a waivered candidate, there was no direct path to special operations."

Contrary to conventional wisdom, the military doesn't take everyone who tries to enlist. Like most modern employers, they do background checks. Any kind of criminal record can prevent an applicant from serving. But in many cases the Army will grant a waiver so the applicant can serve. Even though Duztin didn't get to follow his original special forces dream, he still excelled. It helped that from the start he was comfortable with the military hierarchy and discipline.

"My father and a lot of my family had a military background. My father was strict with discipline because he didn't want me to turn out like him, so in my home growing up, it was: *Yes sir, no sir. Yes ma'am, no ma'am.* So transitioning to military service was easy for me. Some people were appalled at a non-commissioned officer screaming in their faces. The yelling didn't bother me. The aggressiveness didn't bother me."

Neither did the physical rigors, which Duztin considered a fun challenge. "The military does a great job of grouping people according to physical levels in basic training. In my case they put me with other super physically fit, super motivated individuals who are pushing you to run harder, go faster, jump higher. I loved being pushed by every single person every day. It's really neat, and the outcome is amazing."

After advanced infantry training Duztin was assigned to a regular army unit, where they were asked if anyone was interested in being a sniper. "I was in the back and said: *Me! I want that!* In the whole company nobody else raised their hand. The first sergeant asked me why I wanted to be a sniper. I told him to serve my country and because I thought I'd be great at it."

And he was. Duztin made it onto a sniper team then worked his way up to a team leader. "Being on a sniper team fit my personality. And it fit everything I believed the military was to a T. I ate, slept, and shit military service and training, and I gained a lot of experience. But when it came time to reenlist, I had to decide how I wanted to move forward. Did I want a military career or something else? What was I after? What were my goals?"

On one side, the military was familiar and comfortable. "I knew what it was. I understood the military-industrial complex. Also, the government pays for your house, and you earn enough money to live happily and have a lot of security. And that's great for some people."

But Duztin wanted something different. "I had this drive to accomplish more. I had already dabbled in business. I had already seen that I had the ability to go out and change the world. I didn't have to settle."

While on missions Duztin had met a lot of non-military people involved in government work or the military complex industry and saw there were a lot of opportunities. "I met so many civilians making $300,000 a year. They were able to invest their money into things they wanted and believed in. It made me realize there's so much more. So even though I had the drive to go to Ranger school or test my luck on special forces assessment and selection, I had to look at my options objectively."

For all his abilities Duztin knew there were no guarantees of getting into special operations. There was always the risk of injury or simply not making the cut. But even if he did make it, Duztin realized he wanted a different path outside the military.

"There are many things that I would have accomplished had I stayed in," he says. "But I wanted to change the world. When I was in combat, I

saw friends killed in action. Because of their sacrifices I was graced with the ability to come home. Not only is that a blessing, it's a gift. It was also a loud and profound message: *Hey; you're here for a reason. You didn't get killed overseas. You came home. You better go out there and do something to change the world for the better.* The least that I can do with the gift they gave me is to live my life in a way they would be proud of. That's my new mission in life and why I got into security."

While the definition of security is protecting people or things, Duztin approaches it from a different perspective, greatly informed from his sniper training. He sees it as risk management.

"There are two different sides of the world. You have order, which is what we know and control, and we have chaos. The best way we mitigate chaos is through risk management, which is based on intelligence, training, learning, assessment, planning. Sniper teams operate under small unit tactics. We have the ability to move fast and make decisions on the go. The number one ability needed for a sniper team to succeed is the ability to plan and assess risk. In the same way, security is training people to assess risk in real-time, being able to change operational procedures on the fly to respond to the chaos of the world is imperative. Security isn't just putting a uniform on someone. It's much more."

But knowing what direction you want to go doesn't mean you'll get there right away. When Duztin got out of the Army, he went home to spend time with his father.

"He had terminal stage four lung cancer, and the doctors gave him weeks, months I said: *Look, Dad, I'll take care of you; whatever you need I'll be here.*"

Needing to provide some type of income, Duztin took a job at a manufacturing company called American Well Control, digging grease—shoulders deep—out of oilfield frac valves eighty-plus hours a week. It was labor-intensive work, made more challenging in the Texas heat and humidity. Even after his dad passed away, Duztin stayed at the company and was promoted to a welder, doing work reminiscent of his metal fabrication business from when he was eighteen.

"It was a nice position but so monotonous," Duztin says. "I felt like a cog in a machine. I wasn't using the gift of sacrifice I'd been given to its full potential. So I would regularly go to the company president and ask: *Hey, what are you up to? What are you doing? What can I do to help? I could be of more value to this organization than just sitting there with a welding hood on.* I was ignored for quite some time," he says with a laugh.

Then one day it came up that Duztin was a military veteran. It turned out the president's son was an Army Ranger. That was enough of a connection that the executive finally pulled out Duztin's résumé and offered him the job of helping develop one of their field offices in Pennsylvania.

"The next day I was on a plane to Williamsport," Duztin says. "I was deeply driven to make the most of the opportunity and eventually took over business development. I hadn't known there was a job where you took clients out and developed relationships on someone else's dime. It was a lavish life, getting paid to play golf, eat delicious food, and build business relationships. And I enjoyed it because I love getting to know people. I wasn't just building business relationships; I was cultivating friendships. They cared about me, and I cared about them."

Duztin thrived and amassed an enormous book of business throughout the Northeast United States. During that time he met a beautiful woman and became a father of two. But the relationship ended under the strain of his job's demands and other issues.

"It was a punch to the heart for everyone involved," he says. "I had always said the one thing I was going to do right in life was raise my children better than I was raised because I got the crap end of the stick. So now I was in a situation where my decisions had affected my children. I had to re-evaluate."

After some soul-searching Duztin concluded that for as great as it had been to live a high-flying corporate life, it had gotten in the way of his true purpose. "I'd been distracted from my gift, from what I can truly do in the world. It was a gut check to refocus. So around 2011 I started kicking around ideas of how I could use my military leadership skills and the business skills I'd developed throughout my life and came up with a security company."

When he founded RiP his goal wasn't simply to make money off Corporate America. "I needed to do this for the right reasons. I need to use my gift to change the world for the better, to encourage people to make better decisions, to teach people to be better. I want them to stop getting frustrated with life and petty things. Don't lose track of why we have our foundations. Always be humble and respect the gift that was given to you so you can succeed in life. I believe focusing on improving every day can ultimately change the world for the better. I believe that you can encourage people to be better versions of themselves. And I want to use this platform to accomplish that."

Personal purpose and company core values aside, for a business to succeed, it generally needs a value proposition that attracts clients by setting it apart from the competition. But as Duztin notes, security is a dynamic and far-reaching industry, so apples to apples comparisons don't always apply.

"Do I have competition? There are national security organizations that have universal pricing contracts with major corporate infrastructures, so when you look at it that way, yes, we do have competition. But RiP is successful because I have a deep understanding of

security operations. I study it intricately. I have been in many high-risk environments and can speak on the reality of dangerous situations and risk."

RiP's team also brings a lot of individual experience to the table in areas beyond traditional personal security. "We don't just have one company," Duztin explains. "We actually have five companies. We have an instruction and training group. We have RIP USA equipment rentals. We have a consulting division that provides health, safety, environmental, and security support for high-value infrastructure development. And we have RIP Aviation that conducts an enormous amount of high-level drone operations. So do we have competition? Yes and no. We have competition overcoming old school security mentalities, but we don't necessarily have competition doing what we do."

As a result, RiP has grown much more rapidly than Duztin assumed it would, but he wasn't caught flat-footed. "Because of the leadership experience I took away from the military, command and control are a huge part of my skill set. I developed the organization with a scalable leadership platform. So when we've needed to rev up, we were able to almost seamlessly, and we've had some amazing successes with some very large corporations. And in my best estimation, that's an actual value statement. That's tangible. In my opinion, that's success."

The many detours Duztin's professional life took before arriving at RiP taught him more than relationship building and organizational strategy. It also clarified the importance of self-awareness.

"You have to first break down what is valuable to you," he says. "I've learned that the things in life that truly reward you with joy and happiness and success are things of moral fiber—not money, greed, or power. If you want to truly succeed, never attempt to do it on a weak foundation of insignificant, frivolous desires. Do it for a reason, for a purpose. I encourage leaders to use morality. Use love, compassion, and consideration toward the people in your organization when making decisions. Truly care for your subordinates."

Duztin notes that too often people with minimal leadership skills are placed in positions of power. "A true leader cares about the people beneath them. Leads them in the right direction. Leads them to their own success, whether it's with you or another company. If you have a platform to lead from, if someone puts you on a stage, use it for good. Do not use it for superfluous desire or selfishness. Succeeding as an entrepreneur can't be done out of the need for the dollar. It has to be for the right reasons. The world needs more leaders who are going to make the right decisions, even when times get tough. Simply put, lead with your heart."

Sometimes entrepreneurial inspiration comes in an unexpected bolt of Eureka lightning, other times after years of mental tinkering and refining. But occasionally, not finding what you want on store shelves can be an effective motivator for taking a start-up plunge. For Sol-ti founder Ryne O'Donnell, it was the lack of high-quality, healthful food when flying around the country as a twenty-three-year-old sales account executive for a technology company that prompted him to take an unexpected career pivot.

"I would travel a lot and really noticed a difference in my cognitive function and energy levels when I had access to high-quality, organic plant-based food," Ryne says. "I would buy juice and smoothies sold in plastic bottles when I landed in Denver, San Francisco, or JFK and was underwhelmed. It wasn't very tasty or fresh. I just thought: *Why aren't these in glass? Why aren't they organic? Man, somebody must be able to do it better than this.* So that's where the idea began."

Founded in 2014, Sol-ti eventually introduced the first organic, glass bottled, light-filtered living beverages on the market, driven by Ryne's belief that finding fresh and natural beverages should be easy and his passion for healthy living and sustainability, which sculpts the company's culture and vision. "We use only the highest quality, non-genetically modified organic produce, superfoods, and herbs—locally grown whenever possible—to create an unpasteurized, organic, living beverage line at an accessible price point," he says. "Each beverage is an alchemy of fresh, organic ingredients with very real benefits for your well-being: energy, positivity, and health. While other beverage companies use petroleum-based plastic packaging, we bottle our products in glass for purity and taste."

Now sold through retailers such as Publix, Safeway, Target, Walmart, and Whole Foods, Sol-ti grew 152 percent in 2019 and is on pace to match that growth trajectory in 2020. But beyond profit, as a company Sol-ti also measures its success based on how it positively transforms the community and planet. To that end Sol-ti uses glass bottles, aluminum caps, silicone seal gaskets, and recycled cardboard case packaging. A fundamental part of its brand is encouraging consumers to "think about their purchase choices and make conscious decisions, both for their own health and the health of the Earth."

In a post-COVID-19 world, health and sustainability have become more of a focal point for many people across the globe, so in that regard Ryne's vision now seems especially prescient. But in 2013 when he parted ways with his day job to pursue a new career path, products like Sol-ti were still consigned to specialty shops.

Ryne's first foray into health and wellness was to develop a mobile app that enabled users to find health food and juice bars. "By then I was obsessed with this juice thing, so through the app you could send an order to a juice bar or restaurant for either delivery or take-out and pay for it. I worked on that project for six months right after leaving the technology company, but it didn't go anywhere, and I lost fifty grand. I didn't use any investor money. I did take one check from an investor but never cashed it. He was very pleased and ended up investing in Sol-ti," Ryne says.

Despite that loss, Ryne was still well-positioned as far as personal finances. He says he'd been making a healthy six-figure salary at the tech company and had always been a saver.

Ryne O'Donnell

"I started working when I was fifteen, and between then and the time I departed from the sales job, I saved up about $250,000. I did not party. I didn't spend any money on alcohol or drugs. I didn't go out clubbing. I put that money in the bank and ended up putting most of it into the company except for taking out $60,000 to buy a small farm in Costa Rica. It was super expensive to own property in California. But I figured if I lost everything in the start-up, I could go sleep in a tent on my farm in Costa Rica, eat bananas, pick myself up, and figure out where to go from there. That was my legitimate Plan B."

To optimize his resources, Ryne completely changed his lifestyle. As a young tech exec, he had enjoyed the typical creature comforts of a well-compensated twentysomething.

"I lived in a house by myself in Newport Beach. I drove a BMW. I sailed boats every week. But as soon as I moved on from that job, I cut back on everything. I sold my BMW and bought a $2,800 1996 BMW 318ti. I am moved out of the house and into a studio apartment for $1,200 a month. I stopped eating at restaurants. I no longer sailed or went skiing. I got my monthly expenses down to around three thousand dollars. I had to because I was all in."

He started his company in Orange County, moving it to San Diego early on, which had its pros and cons. He said the upsides were the weather, the health food movement, and the yoga movement.

"It's a vibrant community that was evolving and growing. It offered a combination of beach and nature along with business opportunities. The industrial parks were within close proximity to the beach cities, which meant that professional talent was abundant."

The downside was the local water supply. "It had a high amount of total dissolved solids, heavy metals, and chemicals." All the more reason to develop an organic, healthy beverage.

From the beginning Ryne had a clear vision of the product he wanted to create and for it to be bottled in glass. But finding a way to actually do it would take a lot of technological trial and error because if you sell something that's genuinely fresh off the tree that doesn't have a laundry list of additives, shelf life—or lack thereof—is an issue.

"Yes, that was one of the major challenges we had," Ryne says. "When I started the company, then called Shakti, our shelf life was five to seven days. I rented a kitchen by the hour and would make juice from 8:00 p.m. to 1:00 in the morning. Those were the only hours I could afford the kitchen, and doing it then also meant the juice was the freshest."

After juicing he'd go home and sleep until 6:00 a.m. Then he'd load an ice chest into his car and deliver the juice to local stores. "Eventually I hired a few people to do the juicing, which freed me up to focus on more sales, paperwork, and accounting. As the business started to grow, I bought a little van then a refrigerated box truck. At one point we had seven trucks."

But any expansion was limited because of the product's one-week shelf life. "We would go to every store every week, so we could really only serve Southern California. I was set on having the juice in glass from the beginning, but we couldn't preserve it, and we were losing money like crazy because of the short shelf life and the cost of the product. So I was really at a crossroad."

Pressed juice companies often use high-pressure processing (HPP), which kills harmful bacteria and extends the shelf-life for several weeks, but that process uses plastic bottles, which was a non-starter for Ryne. He needed to come up with a first of its kind processing technique. Even though he had worked as a salesman, Ryne was no desk jockey by nature.

He'd been mechanically inclined since his youth.

"I was obsessed in terms of cars," he says. "I had pretty good technical acumen and started rebuilding cars when I was about fifteen years old. I started buying broken down Audi and Porsche cars, took apart engines, transmissions, turbochargers, suspension systems, and electronic systems, fixed everything, put it back together, then sold the refurbished cars."

With that understanding of machinery and technology, Ryne set out to identify a system that could better preserve the juice. "While researching I came across information on UV light filtration, which had been used in water, beer, and apple cider for a while," he says. "I thought if it could be used with cider, why couldn't it be used for juice and living beverages as well?"

But when Ryne contacted some experts at Cornell University, they told him unequivocally that it wouldn't work for his type of juice—especially something like a nice citrus juice or a green juice. He persisted and worked with Tatiana Koutchma, an expert in food safety engineering and one of the top scientists in UV light filtration in the world.

"I finally was able to engineer a machine with UV tubes in a certain configuration that took the shelf life from seven days to about twenty days. And when you drank it on day eighteen, it tasted like day two or three. It was crazy. We knew we had found something."

Not only did UV light filtration offer a nutritionally superior product to HPP, the process also allowed for the use of glass bottles—the ultimate win-win for Ryne. But he wasn't ready to stop at a three-week shelf life. He started targeting other factors that contributed to beverages spoiling. One was that the vessel needed to be sterile.

"When any plastic or glass bottle comes out of the dishwasher, it's clean, but it's not sterile; it still has microbes on the inside you can't see,"

Ryne explains. "To sterilize a glass bottle, you need to heat it to 180 degrees, then cool the glass down to thirty-five degrees by rinsing it with reverse osmosis water. Now you have a pure vessel to put the juice in. Doing that increased our shelf life to fifty days. And again, on day forty-five it tasted like day three."

Next on his checklist was oxygen. He notes how most bottles are not filled to the top, and that headspace is filled with oxygen. The larger the space, the more oxygen in the bottle, and the faster the juice oxidizes, going flat. Ryne's solution was to fill the bottles to the brim then put the cap on.

"That tweak got us another got another ten days," he says, "and now we were up to sixty days."

Step-by-step Ryne kept perfecting his process until he improved the shelf life to between three and four months, depending on the particular recipe.

"They're overfilled. They're aseptically filled. They're cold filled," he says. "You add all those things up, and you don't have to heat pasteurize it to stay fresh." It took Ryne two years and more than a million dollars to perfect his process. "We had microbiologists and engineers coming in all the time; we did countless tests. And in 2015 we received HACCP certification from the Food and Drug Administration."

According to the FDA, HACCP (hazard analysis and critical control point) is a management system *in which food safety is addressed through the analysis and control of biological, chemical, and physical hazards from raw material production, procurement, and handling, to manufacturing, distribution, and consumption of the finished product.*

"HACCP was a huge milestone for us," Ryne says. "Without that we would not be where we are today."

It led to him rebranding the company name to Sol-ti in 2016 and taking on some private investors—former executives of a brewing company. The boost in capital enabled Ryne to move Sol-ti's production headquarters to a 15,000-square-foot space in the San Diego area that included an eight-tap tasting room where consumers could come in and try all the company's juice, tonics, tea, and other beverages in development. Visitors could also watch the entire production process behind a glass observation window, similar to what consumers can experience at a brewery, but which was novel for a non-alcoholic beverage company.

"Juice is very much of a closed-door operation; it's all done behind the scenes as compared to, say, beer, which is very open," Ryne says. "We wanted to connect the dots in terms of showing people where organic comes from, how gentle we are in the process, and how we bottled in our facility. For us it was all about transparency, and the tasting room was a way to show consumers how we make our product and to be very open about it."

By that time Ryne says Sol-ti had two hundred accounts, including with many of Southern California's major grocery stores, yoga studios, and well-regarded shops like Mothers Market and Kitchen, Bristol Farms, and Lazy Acres. In 2017 Southern Pacific Whole Foods stores started carrying Sol-ti products, and the company's future was looking bright. But for a while it seemed Ryne would not be around to enjoy the fulfilled fruits of his juice labors because the company was running out of money, the bane of most start-ups.

"It's not a good place to be," he says. "The most difficult part of being an entrepreneur, by far, is managing cash flow. When you get to a positive EBITDA—earnings before interest, taxes, depreciation, and amortization —it's a beautiful thing. But in September 2016, we were not there. I was in between a rock and a hard spot. So in November I was forced to sell my majority stake in the company, retaining 20 percent but no longer running the company. I said: *Well, you guys are going to run the company. I've done all I can.* I basically became the silent partner."

Ryne implemented Plan B, and a month later packed his bags and moved to his farm in Costa Rica. Within two months he started getting calls from the management team and from some of his investors.

"They told me something wasn't right with the company, and it seemed to be going downhill. The new majority owners agreed to let me come back and run the company for thirty days. So I flew back to California to try and keep the company from going out of business."

It was soon clear to Ryne that the majority owners were no longer interested in running it. Their experience was in manufacturing beer; they weren't used to running a fresh company using a cold chain, and they wanted out. In February 2018 Ryne ended up buying the company back from the majority owners. Or what was left of Sol-ti.

"By then the business was dead on arrival," he says. "So as soon as I bought it back, I called up all my previous managers and said: *Hey, guys; will you come back and help me run the company?* They all said yes. I brought back four of my key guys and gave them a percentage of the company over a four-year vesting schedule. Then we went to work, bringing the company back from the dead."

As to why the previous majority owners had not been able to get Sol-ti over the hump, Ryne suspects it was a matter of focus. "In this industry when a company is in the $1 million to $5 million level, it's really an intense time when the leaders have to live and breathe the brand. I have no doubt those guys were capable of doing it, but they had just sold their beer company for $1 billion in 2015, and they owned 70 percent of the company. So between them they were sitting on close to $700 million cash in their bank accounts. In the end they didn't have the hunger or the drive; they didn't really care about running this little company."

In addition to an unwillingness to put in the grueling hours a start-up requires, they also wanted to minimize overhead. Ryne says one of their first moves as majority owners was to lay off all but a couple of the sales team.

"Prior to that we had at least a dozen. Then all of a sudden the sales team is no longer there. The recurring orders like from a Bristol Farms would still come in, but nobody was driving sales. No one was going into the field making sure the shelf looked good. There was no more proactiveness. So the company's revenue went from $240,000 a month to $110,000 a month. Within five months of cutting the sales force, our revenue was down 50 percent."

Having been through building from scratch before, resurrecting Sol-ti was a little easier the second time around although Ryne says it was still a grind getting the distribution needed. "We were already in Whole Foods and all the markets in Southern California, but we weren't in these stores nationally, and we really needed to change that situation. So the director of sales and I got on a plane and flew around the country, visiting all the top retailers and got commitments from Target, Whole Foods, Walmart, Publix, and Safeway."

Orders for the newly signed retailers and distributors began in 2019. Sol-ti went from $1.4 million in sales to a $6 million run rate by October 2019. Finally, Sol-ti was in the black. It was a slow swell Ryne says he had always been preparing for.

"If you're running a company just to make a living, you can start making profit right away, but those companies are impossible to scale. If you're running it to become a national and international company, there's no way you can make a significant amount of money until you're doing $5 or $10 million a year because the operating costs are so high in the beginning. That's why so many beverage companies fail. They get off the ground then realize how capital-intense the business is, and they can't make it. So from 2014 to 2019 we lost money every single quarter. Then suddenly you go from losing money one month to profiting $100,000 the next. Then if you keep focused, in one year the company can make seven figures in profit because it scaled with financial responsibility."

Even though he was back in charge at Sol-ti, Ryne continued living in Costa Rica full time. He established a Sol-ti company office, and there is a marketing department based there as well. Ryne also runs a real estate development company he founded called Permaculture Planet, which works to reforest overgrazed and degraded land in Costa Rica.

"We're reforesting land with edible fruit tree systems and building natural houses on the land with nice features like pools so that people can live in tune with nature while also living a modern lifestyle."

Ryne has a nursery on-site at one of his properties and grows the trees from saplings, grafting them at about six months old. Depending on the soil fertility, they'll bear fruit between three and five years.

"It's a lot easier growing the trees here than in California," he says. "It's a much faster life cycle."

Ryne also notes that compared to a consumer, packaged goods company like Sol-ti, running Permaculture Planet is relatively not very time-consuming. "It's a walk in the park because after buying the land we have general contractors who build the house and a general manager for the farms that implements the fruit trees systems. So even though they're larger projects and take more time, there are less day-to-day transactions with customers. My role is more the vision, approving the design, and project management."

He estimates he still devotes 80 percent of his working hours to Sol-ti, putting in fifty to sixty hours a week. "But it's way more fun now. I'm working on new product development, marketing, social media, and our e-commerce is really on the rise. I have a great team at Sol-ti. Rob Paladino is our president. He came from PepsiCo and WTRMLN WTR and has a lot of experience growing beverage companies. So I have a really good operating partner there."

Just as important is the team they've assembled. "Every founder dreams of finding team members that they can have take ownership of their responsibilities and actions and be an extension or better than them," Ryne says. "But that's hard, especially for young companies. We've had a turnover of more than one hundred people since we started in 2014 to find the very best people. Our management team today is the culmination of vetting and empowering the right people to lead our organization, which plays a huge role in our current success."

Sol-ti's management structure is especially important because the company's CEO lives way out of town, as in another country. Beyond the professional challenges that entails, a lot of Americans might suffer some personal culture shock uprooting themselves for another country. But Ryne says he found the transition to Central America a smooth one. He and his life partner's parents... not so much.

"Looking back on it, I guess it was kind of a risky move and can see why my mom and Lindsay's parents were questioning us moving to Costa Rica," he says with a laugh. "But for Lindsay and me it was fairly seamless. We speak Spanish, and I had visited Costa Rica many times before and liked the people and the culture. I thought it was adventurous, and now we're very integrated. We employ five or six people full-time and have about twenty contractors who build the houses and implement the permaculture systems, so the community loves us. And we treat them as we would treat friends and family."

A lot of Ryne's time at Sol-ti is spent looking for new products that fit with and advance the brand, such as the SuperShot line the company introduced in 2019, two-ounce wellness shots that come in assorted varieties including turmeric and ginger, and the HEMP+Tea line consisting of organic cold brew tea with 20mg hemp.

Hemp+Tea line

"As of 2020 there are three product lines and about twenty different individual products within those three lines," Ryne says. "I oversaw those three lines personally. I'm the guy in the kitchen figuring out the recipes with my production manager while also listening to the sales and marketing teams and getting their feedback then tweaking the ingredients to make it better and come up with the final recipe."

The next steps are to produce a small run of the new product then send it to a retailer like Mother's Market to see if it generates consumer interest. They use that feedback to tweak the recipe some more, then do another run and sent that to a different retailer. Once they are satisfied with the refinements, it's ready for wider release. Ryne notes that Sol-ti also sells accessories such as insulated glass bottles with a tea infuser, Sol-ti organic clothing and apparel by Patagonia, and are working to develop food products and supplements.

"Some new items we're working on will be plant-based organic, raw, vegan, and delicious. Here in Costa Rica there's a robust supply chain of ginger, coconut, macadamias, cashews, and exotic fruits that can be used. It's really fun."

There aren't many founders who get the opportunity to come back to their company once they sell it. Nor do many guide their company from a different country. But while Ryne's experience has been singular, the fundamental lessons he's learned in growing Sol-ti are universal for all would-be entrepreneurs.

"A lot of people who want to start companies put their idea on a spreadsheet then put it on a PowerPoint. They write a business plan. I think all that's great to a certain extent and many things I did. But at some point you have to take action and start."

Ryne says had he taken a perpetual planning approach to his mobile app, he could have spent two years on his mobile app and not let it go. "But I went with it, and within six months it was released. So my advice is to just go out and sell your product to someone because if you can't do that, it's never going to be viable. And if it doesn't sell, that's okay. Get feedback as fast as you can then take action immediately on it to make adjustments and improve."

Going hand-in-hand with that is making sure you have a cash reserve. "You need to be able to live without an income for twelve or eighteen months. If you can do that, then you'll have the time to focus on the startup and figure out how to develop a product that you can sell. Enjoy the journey!"

Well into the twentieth century, a majority of prospective employers sought workers through newspaper listings. And a majority of prospective employees found work through word of mouth, spotting a help wanted sign in a storefront window, or by reading the local want ads. There was a lot of hit or miss in that system. It wasn't until World War II that the first staffing agencies emerged, finding an opportunity in helping fill positions from factory worker to bank teller vacated by the men and women serving in the war effort.

Today while the main purpose of the industry remains acting as a middleman between employers and employees, making it easier for both sides to find a match, there is now some differentiation. Generally speaking, an employment agency specializes in placing individuals in long-term positions. When contacted by employers with positions to fill, the agency selects a qualified individual from their pool of prospects and sends them for an interview.

A staffing agency mainly specializes in providing temporary workers for companies looking to cover for an employee on vacation or out on sick leave. Staffing agencies also provide seasonal help, such as during Christmastime. Again, they send a qualified individual from a pool of pre-screened prospects.

Recruitment firms tend to fill higher-level openings. That can be business management and executive-level positions, or it can be for someone with specialized technical qualifications, such as in computer programming or engineering. In the case of Shurig Solutions Inc. (SSI), an affiliate of MRINetwork, its specialty is helping fill positions in the medtech and pharmaceutical industries.

Founder Darwin Shurig says, "We focus on regulatory affairs, quality, and engineering within the medical industries. We started in medical device but added pharma in year three and are probably 70 percent medical device at this point. And we've grown pretty substantially over the last five years, doubling in revenue in 2016, 2017, and 2019."

Darwin started the company with a vision to bring value to candidates and companies in the medical device industry through both integrity to the process and increased efficiency. He says Shurig Solutions is committed to a strong relationship-driven approach that combines best-in-class recruiting practices and continuous training to provide an exceptional level of service to every client and candidate.

"We've developed a system that helps clients identify, attract, and retain the top talent in the industry more efficiently. Our process prevents candidates from doing interviews that don't match their career interests and prevents hiring managers from wasting time with prospects who don't have the right skills, experience, or fit for their culture. Every day we help our clients locate and place that 20 percent of the available workforce who make 80 percent of the impact on a business, and our offer acceptance rate has averaged 91 percent since 2015."

While Darwin is humbled by his company's success, he admits that he never expected to have *recruiter* on his résumé. "If someone had told me six years ago that I'd own a recruiting firm, I would have probably hurt myself laughing at them because my perspective of the recruitment industry was not particularly positive."

And there wasn't much in his professional background to suggest his career path would wind its way to recruitment. "I'm a registered

Darwin Shurig

respiratory therapist," Darwin says. "I started in the clinical world, doing patient care, critical care, ICU, burn unit, acute care, peds—a lot of different areas."

It wasn't so much being a jack of all trades as it was being intellectually restless. "There are a lot of things that I find interesting," he says with a laugh. "I like new things. I'm not the kind of person who wants to go to the same place every year for vacation for example. I don't want to go to Florida and sit on the beach during spring break. I've been to Florida and sat on the beach. I want to go to Italy or Thailand. I like meeting new people. I like learning new things and want to be in a situation where I am growing personally and professionally."

He also liked having a bit more wind beneath his wings, which is what led him into other aspects of clinical application from sub-acute care to home care. "Though I liked a lot of aspects relevant to patient care, I really didn't like being stuck in the hospital for thirteen hours at a time. With home care you're going out in the world to see patients. And there's a little bit more freedom to it, which better fit my personality."

A stroke of serendipity led to Darwin's pivot to sales. One day one of the marketers at the healthcare company he was working for was let go, and the branch manager called Darwin into his office and offered him the job after the manager's wife told him that she thought Darwin would be a great fit.

It wasn't as much of a left turn as a course correction. "I had sold cutlery and cookware for two summers in college to make money instead of having a hard labor summer job. I've cleaned out horse barns, worked in factories, and de-tasseled corn. Sales was more challenging mentally, it paid a lot better, and it fit my personality; I like people."

Even so he hesitated—until he heard how much he'd make on commissions. "That I understood, and I liked the ability to make more with a bonus opportunity, and essentially that's how I moved into full-time sales. I enjoyed it. In that work you're reaching out to people you don't know and building relationships, trying to sell a product or service based on customer needs, mentoring others once you're a manager, and trying to empower people."

Even if the position hadn't come along when it did, Darwin says he'd always considered clinical healthcare work as more of a steppingstone than a permanent vocation. And once working in sales, he went back to school and earned his MBA with the idea of owning his own business ... someday.

For the next decade-plus, sales led Darwin to sales leadership, marketing, contract negotiations, and business development. "I saw that as an avenue where I could bring more value to my family, where I could make more money and not just simply trade hours for dollars. Additionally, I liked the mental strategy, preparation, and execution of a game plan that goes into the process. When you're in a hospital setting, to make more money you have to work more hours—holidays, weekends. And in sales I didn't have to be on call anymore."

A dozen years into his sales career, McKesson, the oldest and largest healthcare company in the United States, acquired the company Darwin was working at. "After a large integration they eventually gave me an exit package, and along with about two hundred others, I was downsized," he says. "That gave me an opportunity to evaluate my career and determine what I wanted to do."

Years earlier while on his honeymoon in Italy, Darwin had met Dave Dart, partner of the Morisey-Dart Group, an executive recruitment firm.

They had stayed in touch, mostly on social media, so when he found himself at a professional crossroads, Darwin reached out.

"I wasn't even exactly sure what Dave worked on position-wise, but I thought he had some focus on medical devices," he says with a laugh. "But I said: *Hey, if you have anything in clinical sales leadership let me know.* Dave said their company didn't do a lot of that, but he promised to see if they had anything for me."

Two days later, while he was working an agency shift at the hospital as a therapist, Darwin received a text from Dave: *We need to talk.* Darwin learned during their next conversation that Dave's company was a franchisee of Management Recruiters International (MRI).

"He shared with me how it worked, and I explored the idea of starting my own business as an MRI franchise. At the same time during that process, a lot of opportunities were coming my way. I interviewed for different positions that were interesting to me, and it was getting close to where I was probably going to get a couple of offers. But after I went to what they called discovery day, I came away from it realizing I just did not want to go back into the corporate world. I didn't want to work for somebody else. I wanted the opportunity to build something for my family instead of building revenue for other companies."

The recruitment industry, which generates more than $150 billion a year, certainly offered opportunity. And despite some reservations Darwin harbored based on some past interactions with recruiters, he felt his background in building relationships, bringing people solutions, and mentoring were highly applicable to the industry.

"So I just decided: *Well, I get to choose. I'll be the owner and can decide just not to do those things I didn't like.* In my experiences with recruiters, I felt there hadn't been a lot of value or time put into the interactions; they would try to sell you on the position, or if you didn't exactly fit the job description, you never heard from them again. And oftentimes it was obvious from the conversation that they didn't know much about the company or the industry. It came across as a lack of professionalism or polish."

Darwin made sure he presented a different perception because long-term relationship building is critical. He says the reality facing many companies is that there are more positions to fill than available talent as a rule at least in the areas his firm focuses on. At least 40 to 50 percent of positions open or about to come open aren't even posted.

"The first thing a company tends to do is contact people they know. *Let's ask Sally; she'd be great at this.* But then Sally either doesn't want to commute that far or is happy where she's at or whatever. The executive or manager then goes to HR and explains what they need. So HR places an ad in the paper, on a job site, wherever. But less than 20 percent of the relevant talent pool will actually see those ads."

Darwin notes that most of that 20 percent are people unemployed or unhappy where they are employed. "Not that you can't find the right person for some positions going the ad route, but generally the company ends up fishing in the smallest part of the pond. About 80 percent of the talent we look for is not actively looking; they're what we call passive candidates." In the five years SSI has been in business, the company has never filled a position with someone who responded to an ad or job posting.

Conversely, the company also offers prospects an opportunity to break through overwhelmed human resources departments. "Most people in HR have a lot of responsibilities," Darwin says. "If you're applying to for a position online, you're essentially hoping some HR generalist singles your information out from hundreds of others and is able to glean enough from your résumé in the minute or so they spend looking at it to consider you. And a lot of times cover letters are just completely ignored. It's much better for a candidate to get with a recruiting firm that has a relationship with the hiring manager or has had success partnering with the company. Then instead of your résumé going into a pile, the recruiter can bypass that process and get that information directly to the hiring manager while working in triangulation with HR or talent acquisition, which is more likely to lead to an interview."

It's not unusual for a company to use multiple recruiting firms on contingency to locate talent. That approach makes quality control more difficult.

"From my experience they have no clue what the recruiters are saying to the candidates or how they represent the company in the marketplace," Darwin says. "That is one aspect of recruiting and how companies manage their processes that has amazed me the past five years. Companies spend millions of dollars to position their product, service, or value prop in the marketplace. Why would you then give any recruiter or multiple recruiters the ability to share your value prop based simply on the lowest fee without knowing how they are sharing and protecting that value prop in the marketplace? In this day and age, you shouldn't pay a recruiter to solely find talent; you're paying them to identify the right talent and attract the talent to your value prop while also protecting your image."

Darwin says when he was in sales, he'd get calls from recruiters. "If you weren't interested or you didn't fit what that job description was, they went away pretty quickly. Or you'd have an interview with a recruiter for a position, and they'd tell you: *This could be a great fit*. Then you'd never hear from them again or get any feedback."

From the start Shurig Solutions has made a point to emphasize communication with prospective candidates. "We want them to understand what's positive about the hiring company, the position, and the industry. I think part of the reason that we've been successful is because my goal—and we talk about this every day—is to bring value. If you're pushing candidates towards positions that don't make sense for them, or you're sending your client candidates that don't fit what they're looking for, you're not going to have nine out of every ten offers being accepted over several years as we do for all searches. For engaged or retained searches, we actually have a 100 percent offer acceptance rate over the past three years. The reason we have a good chance of getting to the offer stage and it being a win-win for everybody is our process of specificity and clarity."

Darwin says they work every day to bring both client and candidate value. The emphasis is to build a network, have conversations to understand what people want and what they're interested in, and be a proactive resource for what is happening in the industry.

"If you're focused on them and you're good at sharing the value prop of the client's opportunity, then you can find the right talent and help them explore the opportunity," Darwin says. "That's what works for us. The goal is to bring in three to four candidates with the right skill set that the client will want to talk to. You get enough information, vet it, and then submit it in a way that paints a picture for them of what the candidate has accomplished and who they are, so they know we're not wasting their time. Only one person will get any position, so managing expectations and communication is essential. As long as each person, the candidate, and the hiring manager come away from the interview feeling they haven't wasted their time, then we have done our job well."

Darwin says it's equally important to support each candidate through the process from interview to accepted offer. "That's how we make money.

When the fee is contingent on filling their position, that means if the client doesn't accept any of the candidates, you can spend an awful lot of time working without making any money if you're not careful. It's even trickier when you're on contingency while also competing against other firms for the same candidate pool."

The Shurig family

Recruiters can also work on a retained basis, meaning the recruiter will charge the client an upfront fee to conduct a search. In that case the recruiter operates on an exclusive basis; there is no competition, and the job will generally only be filled through that recruitment company. An engaged search is a cross between contingency and retained. In this agreement a percentage of the fee is paid when the search starts, but the rest of the fee is only paid if a candidate the recruiter has found is placed.

Darwin stresses that even though they only get paid by the company seeking talent, he also considers the candidates his client, although he acknowledges there is a fine line. "The client company pays the bills. That's where we build revenue, so we have to bring them value. But we certainly have the candidates' best interest at heart as well. My goal every single day is to not be a recruiter or a headhunter or whatever terminology you want to use. My goal every single day is to be an agent. To myself I sound like a broken record, but at least ten times a day I say to candidates that our goal is to bring those we engage with value based on their interests."

Even if a candidate turns out not to be the specific fit Shurig Solutions' client is looking for, the time spent getting to know the candidate is never time wasted. "The worst case is we've made a connection, and now I understand what the candidate has to offer, so if I reach out to them again, they know it'll be worth their while, and we won't waste their time. It's important, and I believe candidates appreciate that we aren't selling or pushing anything."

Beyond attention to detail, the company is also differentiating itself through its work ethic. "When I was a teenager my dad told me: *If you work hard in life, you'll beat out 50 percent of the competition; if you work hard and you're honest, you'll beat out 90 percent.* That always stuck with me, and I've tried to share that principle with my children, as well."

Darwin says the recruitment industry is huge and wide-ranging but also very top-heavy in terms of the bigger, retained firms, so it's not easy to break into. "Nobody knows who you are; you have no value prop in the marketplace when you start, and people often don't return your phone calls. Business in general is hard, and 80 percent of companies don't make it past the first two years; in recruiting, four out of five people trying to enter the industry don't make it past the first year because there is a lot of rejection."

Rather than be daunted, Darwin felt challenged. "That was exciting to me, because if I focus on getting better, understanding the industry challenges and direction, I know I will get better because I'm going to do the work, I'm going to invest the time, and I'm coachable. So my perspective was if every year 80 percent of the people I'm competing against go away, that's awesome. Of course, had I known everything I was going to need to learn, everything we'd have to overcome up front, then I'd probably have been in the corner sucking my thumb," he laughs.

One area that was intuitive for Darwin was recognizing the need for interview training. "In my experience most people don't interview people very well. So there are certain aspects of interviewing, both tangible and intangible, that we bring value to the process in support of the candidate. In addition to things like what the hiring manager is looking for and intangibles about the position or company, SSI also helps candidates on how to communicate their success examples more efficiently. We focus on the STAR format: situation, task, action taken, and result. Efficient communication is huge for the positions we're working to fill. I can't tell you how many times I have witnessed talented, good candidates not get an offer because they simply didn't communicate their experience efficiently. The manager needs to get a good feel for a candidate's experience and expertise, so we try to help prepare candidates from that standpoint. Every single time you interact with somebody, you either gain credibility, or you lose it. You either bring value, or you don't bring value. They have to see that you are going to be a good fit, are able to execute, and will ultimately make their life easier."

As the company has grown, the yeoman's work needed to build the business has evolved into a more visionary role. "The first two or three years, we didn't get jobs unless I was on the phone," Darwin says. "They told me: *If you made fifty phone calls a day, this is what most people make.* So my attitude was: *Okay, I'm going to make ninety calls a day then.* Whatever you're telling me I need to do to be successful, I'm going to do at least 25 percent more."

Now that Shurig Solutions is evolving, Darwin doesn't have to be on the phone all day and can put his energies elsewhere. "Now we have agreements in place. We're getting retained projects. We're getting engaged director-level searches with money upfront, so we can be more selective of what we work on. The first three years, nobody gave me money upfront for anything," he laughs.

As part of his longer-term vision, Darwin plans to bring on more staff that will specialize: one person for quality, one who will only do marketing positions, someone to focus solely on IT and software development, which is a rapidly growing area within the medical device industry. "Because we already have the agreements in place, and we've earned a bit of reputation, we can take those processes and that value and put it into another aspect. Another pillar within the same building, so to speak."

SSI is also adding more automations to their marketing strategies for increased scale. "We've invested in equipment and additional tools to start educational webinars with experts in regulatory affairs, quality, engineering, and other areas that will bring relevant information to people growing their career in the niche. SSI invested substantially in equipment and adding the right medium for 2020 to start these, which have been extremely well received to date. Additionally, SSI is gathering extensive marketing content that can be reused strategically with small to medium-sized enterprises in the industry."

The company's continued growth also allows Darwin to make good on a promise he made when he took the entrepreneurial plunge. "Starting the business was scary," he admits. "And I wasn't sure until the last minute if I was really going to do it instead of taking one of the jobs I was going to be offered. I was the primary breadwinner with three kids. It meant not just giving up a guaranteed six-figure income but also investing a large amount of my retirement money—which my accountant begged me not to do when I told him what I was considering. And I had no idea how long it would be before I started to make money. And I didn't make any for the first six months, so that was really frightening."

In the end it came down to faith. "That's a big part of who I am, and my mother had a large part in driving that through the seeds she planted. So is charitable work and bringing positive energy to others. So when I decided to go for it, I made a commitment to God that if he would direct me and open the right doors, I would give a portion of every dollar the business made to charity. And that's something we have done and which keeps growing each year. Based on that direction I felt I couldn't fail, like John 14:13-14: *And I will do whatever you ask in my name so that the Father may be glorified in the Son. You may ask me for anything in my name, and I will do it.*"

Starting in 2016, Darwin has gone every year on a mission trip to the Dominican Republic, where they support a Christian school called Freedom International that Jason and Pam Helgeman started in July 2011. Shurig Solutions also supports the Life Center or Apostolate of Divine Mercy in South Bend, Indiana, and founded by  Shawn Sullivan in 2010, which provides women who do not have resources other options besides abortion. And the company also supports a charity in North Carolina that provides horseback riding for kids with disabilities called Brighstar Stables that was established in 2010, owned by his dear friends of more than twenty years, the Glazers. "So giving back has been a big part of our value proposition too, in terms of bringing value to other people," he says.

Darwin is also generous with his experience, willing to share lessons learned on his start-up journey and is often asked by MRI to share his experiences with new owners. "I had always heard that the biggest reasons businesses failed were either people partnered with the wrong people, didn't have the right plan, or they ran out of money. So obviously if you want to start and grow your own company, you need to understand the four Ps of marketing—product, price, promotion, and place—that are relevant to your industry. And the other thing is to identify your value proposition. If you cannot differentiate yourself from the competition while knowing and believing in your why, then you're going to have a hard time making it."

Simply put, due diligence is critical. But so is ability or at least the willingness to spend the time and effort needed to accrue the necessary tools and skill set. "I remember hearing someone once say: *You really shouldn't do things you're not good at. I really wanted to play the piano, so I took lessons for a year, and I was still horrible.* And I laughed because yeah, you can have a great idea, but if you don't have or develop the tools to implement the right plan and to understand the market, you're going to have a hard time being successful."

Above all, Darwin also believes it's important to have an honest conversation with yourself about your motivations to start your own business. "Being an entrepreneur is hard," he says. "It's easy to get distracted; it's easy to get discouraged. My wife, Jamie, has believed in me, supported me, and been understanding through the long days to build the business. Knowing your why is what's going to keep you focused and get you through the challenging times. Every time the business has stalled, or we had issues, it was because I lost focus of why I'm doing it, and my ego got in the way. For me the reason I get up in the morning comes back to the charitable piece, to my family, and making the best use of the gifts God has blessed me with." It also helps to have support at home. "My wife, Jamie, has believed in me, supported me, and been understanding through the long days to build the business."

Darwin jokes that if it weren't for his wife, kids, and faith, "I'd probably be sitting on a couch somewhere. I probably wouldn't have made the commitment to found and grow Shurig Solutions for myself, but I want to bring value to other people. If it weren't for my faith and what I want to do on the charitable side, I'd be fine with how much money we made last year. Material things don't really excite me. I am more interested in experiences and creating memories. My wife and I could afford really nice cars right now, but we don't really care about that. We're fine driving two paid-off cars and having more cash flow. Don't get me wrong; I like nice things, nice meals, and nice trips, but it needs to be about bringing value to others, offering encouragement to others either professionally or in their faith. The fruits come about as a complementary secondary benefit. If I can sponsor four more kids or I can donate $5,000 to Bright Star Stable so they can get another horse giving ten more kids the chance to ride, bringing added value to their lives, that's exciting to me. Creating more opportunities for my kids, that's exciting. It's like Matthew 25:40: *The King will reply, Truly I tell you, whatever you did for one of the least of these brothers and sisters of mine, you did for me."*

At the same time, Darwin is aware charity needs to walk hand-in-hand with humility. "It's not about: Oh, look what I did. And that's a concern for me in doing any sort of promotion including my initial hesitance to be in this book. It can't be about ego. And if it also benefits the business and helps it grow based on bringing true value to others, which in turn will provide more means for charity, then that's pretty cool, and I'm good with it."

The team working

TERA⅃GROUP

The Great Recession that started in 2008 generated widespread economic, social, and political fallout. Lending dried up as banks held onto their cash reserved with a vice-grip that would do Scrooge McDuck proud. People put off having children, with an estimated 500,000 fewer births per year of the recession. And in an effort to prevent the chain of events that torpedoed the economy from happening again, Congress passed the Dodd-Frank Wall Street Reform and Consumer Protection Act.

In a very simple nutshell, the law sought to "promote the financial stability of the United States by improving accountability and transparency in the financial system" by placing strict regulations on lenders and banks. It also created several new agencies to oversee the regulatory processes and implement changes to stop mortgage companies and lenders from taking advantage of consumers. But there was very little simple about complying with the intricacies of Dodd-Frank. So in 2011 Christian Martin co-founded Tera Group to help market participants "meet the regulatory goals of increasing transparency, accountability, and oversight" in the brave new Dodd-Frank world.

"If you want to put someone to sleep at a cocktail party, just bring up Dodd-Frank," Christian says with a laugh. "But I created TeraExchange." the Tera Group's platform that clients trade derivatives on, "as a direct result of the credit crisis."

Prior to founding Tera Group, Christian spent twenty years at Merrill Lynch and five at Bank of America as a fixed income and derivatives trader for emerging market debt. "The unregulated and largely unchecked execution and support of derivatives trading for several decades led to the 2008 credit crisis and likely bought the entire financial system to the brink of collapse," he says. "It can be a bit ponderous to discuss derivatives; however, TeraExchange's central thesis is guided by providing safety and soundness as our main value proposition to this previously underserved space."

A derivative is a financial contract that derives its value from an underlying asset. Derivatives are often used for commodities (oil, gasoline, gold), bonds, interest rates, market indexes, stocks, and currencies, including the US dollar.

Investopedia explains: *Generally belonging to the realm of advanced investing, derivatives are secondary securities whose value is solely based (derived) on the value of the primary security that they are linked to. In and of itself, a derivative is worthless. . . . While a derivative's value is based on an asset, ownership of a derivative doesn't mean ownership of the asset.*

According to the most recent data from the Bank for International Settlements, for the first half of 2019, the total amounts outstanding for contracts in the derivatives market was an estimated $640 trillion. Christian says the US equity market is around $35 trillion.

"Most people have heard of, or are at least familiar with, stocks and bonds. Then there are futures and options, which are still common but are definitely more complicated products and have a smaller number of market participants. Finally, there are swaps and other over the counter (OTC) products listed on TeraExchange. These are the most complicated financial instruments and are limited to institutional market participants only."

Christian explains that for decades these OTC instruments were transacted bilaterally, meaning from one of the big broker-dealers or banks

Christian Martin

directly to an institutional client. There was no central place or exchange for trading in the way people are accustomed to doing with stocks.

"Due to this legacy bilateral execution process, there was no liquidity formation, price discovery, or consistent execution methodology. Most importantly there was increasing counterparty risk as more and more of these bilateral trades accumulated on participants' balance sheets. It is this very point, counterparty risk, that opened the process up to what took place throughout the credit crisis. It was a daisy chain of interconnected risk whereby if any of the major pieces in the chain faltered, the entire succession was at risk."

He says Dodd-Frank—and by extension, TeraExchange—attempted to address the weak spots in the old status quo with the goal of ensuring the financial system does not repeat the mistakes that were profoundly revealed during the Great Recession. "Safety and soundness, common-sense guidelines around reporting, transparency, and equitable markets are some of the tenants of what a post-Dodd-Frank financial universe is looking to incorporate and core to TeraExchange's mission. Considering the scale and scope of this $600 trillion-plus marketplace, it's certain there are iterative steps still needed. It's impossible to think of this as a finished process, but the important first steps have started."

Of course, to the casual observer Wall Street has often seemed like a financial Wild West. Back in the 1980s Michael Milken made high-risk junk bonds—loans made to companies with a higher likelihood of defaulting—a money machine for his company, investment bank Drexel Burnham Lambert. Then he ran afoul of the SEC and went to jail, and Drexel went bankrupt. But even after that scandal, little seemed to change as far as practices and oversight.

"While they're different vehicles, the issue always comes down to there's a reason it was called a credit crisis, not a liquidity crisis—you couldn't trust the creditworthiness of your counterparty," Christian says. "In the case of Drexel Burnham, investors thought the bonds were a relatively safe way to make a little bit more money than they could by buying a bond from GE. But it all comes down to getting money back. So if you don't put that big warning sign on that bond with a low rating saying: *Hey, there's a really good chance this will default* that's a problem. And when it does default, all kinds of bad stuff start to happen. So that was a credit story. In the 2008 recession it was the same thing but in a much, much bigger scenario because of how huge the global derivatives market is. Hedge funds, asset managers, Sallie Mae, Freddy Mac, and even nations all used derivatives to hedge their risk, and they all did it in the same fashion: directly with the banks, with no reporting, no intermediary, no regulatory oversight, no rules of the road. The on-ramp and off-ramp didn't even exist."

Of course, banks had spent a lot of money on lobbyists who successfully convinced legislators that regulations were not needed. But as Christian notes, the system supporting the marketplace, for the most part, worked for decades—until it didn't.

"Back in the days of Alan Greenspan and intermittently over the years the regulators, the banks and biggest broker-dealers would engage in analysis and dialogue about what was the correct way forward regarding the trading of these OTC instruments. The choices repeatedly came down to who was best suited to manage the marketplace's risk. The regulators and legislators sided with the banks, which were good at forming beachheads to promote and effectuate their abilities to pioneer and innovate in this space," Christian says. "But ultimately the process had issues with scale and other ever-increasing variables, so by the mid-2000s you had to wonder if the tail was wagging the dog."

Meaning, were the OTC derivative markets more important than the underlying instrument they derived their value from? In the end, all the mattered was curing the problem and getting the financial system on firm footing as bank after bank was running into solvency issues.

"The daisy chain," Christian says, "was surely broken."

During the recession Lehman Brothers filed for bankruptcy, Bear Stearns collapsed and was eventually bought out for pennies on the dollar, and Wachovia Bank disappeared. Bank of America bought a floundering Merrill Lynch. It became clear these were not independent, isolated occurrences.

"The thread that connected all these venerable generationally successful companies was the OTC derivative exposure they had to one another," Christian says. "The strength of the entire banking system's daisy chain was only as strong as the weakest link, and there were weak links everywhere."

There was a growing fear that banks could start defaulting in a domino effect, so the government bailed them out, believing they were too big to fail.

"Without the benefit of easily accessible—or in some cases any—data to determine the resources any one bank or broker-dealer needed to stay solvent, the solution instead resembled more of a sledgehammer approach," Christian recalls. "The trillion-dollar government bailout of the banks kept the daisy chain intact enough to function. In my opinion even if the bailout wasn't perfect, it was 100 percent needed so that our banking system and economy could survive to see another day."

When Dodd-Frank passed, it basically created a layer of

infrastructure that one would have assumed was already there but wasn't, just like investors take for granted that there are stock exchanges and futures exchanges—central places that balance the risk and create proper safety and soundness.

"As the dust settled post-crisis, Congress looked to institute a framework that would address the issues that had led to multiple banks collapsing and the resulting bailouts," Christian says. "In the spirit of *If it ain't broke, don't fix it,* Congress recognized that the exchange model that had served the stock and futures markets for more than a hundred years functioned well during bull and bear markets alike. Proper reporting, sound risk management, transparency, and healthy objective oversight are fundamental to the exchange model and in large part were what the OTC derivative marketplace needed and what Dodd-Frank provided by instituting the workflows that serviced other asset classes well, hence the formation of TeraExchange, which bases our service model on those same tried and true principals."

#

Around the time the prospects of our banking system imploding were scaring the bejesus out of Wall Street and Main Street alike, a new cryptocurrency called bitcoin that completely bypassed banks was introduced to the world in 2008. By definition, a cryptocurrency  is a digital or virtual currency. Many cryptocurrencies are decentralized networks based on blockchain technology, a distributed ledger enforced by a disparate network of computers. A defining feature of cryptocurrencies is that they are generally not issued by any central or government authority. So if suddenly all the banks defaulted and your ATM no longer dispensed cash or if dollars became worthless, you could use the bitcoin cryptocurrency as a substitute. The creation of bitcoin was driven in part by the prospect of our banking system totally collapsing, a doomsday scenario that had come uncomfortably close to reality in 2008–2009.

"I was introduced to bitcoin in 2013," Christian recalls. "While I was not a domain expert in cryptocurrency by a long shot, I *was* a domain expert in financial marketplaces and very familiar with the use cases for an instrument that possessed the qualities of bitcoin. Bitcoin, other cryptocurrencies, and tokens have evolved and matured a lot since 2015, and are no longer seen as a curiosity. With that maturity comes the need for the same tenants that constitute the baseline for TeraExchange's offering. Safety, soundness, transparency, and common-sense reporting guidelines are crucial to a marketplace where participants can interact with one another in a confident, compliant manner."

While Christian admits he can't predict whether bitcoin or any other crypto offerings will survive in the long haul, he can say that as long as they are relevant variables in the financial landscape, he'll have an opportunity "to provide needed infrastructure to the effort that allows for creativity, price discovery, and innovation, all while promoting well-designed and regulated on-ramps and off-ramps for participants."

He believes the reason bitcoin has captured so much mind share can be explained by another technological artifact—the fax machine. "If you think about it," Christian says, "the first fax machine was totally useless because there was no other machine to fax to or get a fax from. The more the technology was adopted, the more ubiquitous faxes became. Every new fax machine expanded the network, adding value to the first fax machine. This is known as the network effect and is what we also witnessed with bitcoin. The more entrants into the bitcoin network that accept and send bitcoin, the stronger the network has become, making it the leader in the crypto clubhouse."

All bitcoin transactions are recorded on the bitcoin blockchain. About every ten minutes a new block is added with all the transactions that took place since the previous ten-minute block. The entire historical record from the very first bitcoin transaction to the most recent is observable.

Christian notes that even though the American dollar is no longer backed by a tangible asset since we left the gold standard when Nixon was president, our currency works because we believe it works. We trust it to have value. Blockchain is designed to give bitcoin users trust in its value.

"It's up to each individual to decide for themselves if the information they are observing instills enough confidence to transact on the network," he says. "There are other important factors that should ultimately impact the trust decision as well, but access to the fully exposed recorded ledger for every transaction is a unique offering by itself. There are multiple commercial efforts today that are focused on extending blockchain for a myriad of uses separate from its utility as the bitcoin ledger."

Christian says TeraExchange's goal was to list "a fully regulated bitcoin derivative product available for all institutional market participants to trade for hedging and or risk-taking purposes. In late 2014 Tera Exchange became the first regulated platform in the United States to list a bitcoin product for trading. The scale of the legacy products listed for trading on TeraExchange, which included interest rate swaps and credit default swaps, was enormous compared to the nascent bitcoin marketplace; however, the mind share, inquiry, and interest surrounding this new cryptocurrency was unmistakable. We offer solutions that can be shaped to accommodate a nearly limitless number of objectives and strategies. By adhering to the value proposition we offer agility, providing our clients with the highest-quality execution, unmatched reaction to evolving market dynamics, and a truly differentiating advantage."

Pushing the frontiers of finance, I want to allow our clients the ability to produce models with relaxed constraints stripped of limitations, which offer increased utility in a broader set of applications."

Unlike some entrepreneurs who come out of the gate intent on working for themselves, founding Tera Group came about because after a successful career Christian identified an opportunity. "Given my background working in securities, it was really obvious to me that after the credit crisis in 2008, this layer of infrastructure, this exchange model, was a good idea that hit me right in the face. Its time had definitely come."

He says that promoting a more secure, stable financial infrastructure to help prevent anything like the Great Recession's credit crisis again also suited his sensibilities. "That was so devastating across the country in so many different ways to so many people."

He says the marketplace they were targeting is so large that it's difficult to manage on a spreadsheet, but its size was an obvious advantage. "For even a modest percentage of the market share, we could provide a valuable service, get paid for that service, reasonably expect to be a profitable enterprise, and see where it takes us."

Christian believes Dodd-Frank will do well to prevent another credit crisis. "Now, there'll be other crises that are bound to come up and knock us sideways. But this one was a long time coming. And I think the regulators are mostly well-intentioned, smart people trying to do smart things. I know that's not the common way to think of them because they tend to get a bad rap. But in this case, I think they got it right. That doesn't mean I think everything they wrote is perfect, but we're living and breathing and walking through the process with good results."

The years of working at Merrill Lynch and Bank of America prepared Christian for the mental challenge of starting and organizing his own company. "I knew there would be technical subject matters that I would have to be a quick study on or find someone who already was. And that attitude has served me as well as could be."

But he admits there were anxious moments addressing aspects of founding a business he had no depth of knowledge in, such as insurance and technical issues. Dealing with the human aspect was also new.

"So things like human resources, staffing, making sure we hired talented people, and dealing with people when they were having a rough go of it, and doing it all with the knowledge that you have to keep moving forward. You can get knocked sideways a little bit, but you can't go sideways for too long, not in this industry," Christian says. "The finance world is a very hungry, very frisky place for a start-up."

For general consumer goods or services, you build a clientele by appealing to a broad audience. As an institutional-only platform, Tera Group serves a specialized niche, but that doesn't necessarily mean it's a limited market.

"There is an unlimited number of institutions out there that need to traffic in derivatives—all the financial institutions, the biggest government-sponsored entities, and a good bunch of asset managers and insurance companies as well."

So knowing the target wasn't that hard, but Christian says the meetings in the early days were more about educating clients: *Here's what Dodd-Frank means to you. Here's what our value proposition is as a platform. Here are some competitors that might be good for you in some circumstances, and our value prop might be good in others.*

"Obviously we want them to become a commercial client of ours, but in the interim we believe in the virtuous cycle of helping out and believing in the network effect of nurturing prospects and clients so that one day they become true partners. Either way we were in one of the rare circumstances where regulation was a tailwind and not a headwind because in a post-

Dodd-Frank world, these derivative instruments were going to be mandated to trade on these regulated platforms. In a lot of cases, all we had to do was just avail ourselves to the client looking for that solution. It was good timing."

Christian believes that had Tera Group started before Dodd-Frank, it would have been just as good an idea. But implementing it would have been challenging.

"These are such intricate processes that had been in place for decades," he notes. "It would have been very difficult to go in and say: Okay, we think we're ultimately going to save you a lot of money by providing you transparency, standardization, and regulatory solutions that you'll benefit from if you just give us a shot. It would have been hard for an established government client to turn around and say: *Yeah, that sounds like a good idea* because they've built an infrastructure around doing it the old way that had been in place forever. But with the force of the law and our platform, we can keep the safety and soundness aspect as a baseline, so the issue isn't the infrastructure anymore, which it was during the credit crisis. And then whether you put on a good trade or don't put on a good trade is a separate story. Again, we're not everybody's solution, and there are strengths and weaknesses to every offering."

As far as direct apples-to-apples competition, Christian says there are a handful of other long-established companies. "They took their franchises and bent them to become compliant with Dodd-Frank. But they didn't change any of their protocols; they didn't do anything different."

The legacy infrastructure players had an enormous advantage because they were installed, so they didn't have to fight for market, relevance, or name recognition. Despite that, Christian notes, "As in sports, I think it's best to press the advantages that you have rather than trying to beat opponents at their own game. We have unique offerings that allow our clients to form certain commercial beachheads that differentiate our offering. We will not be all things to all people, but in a $600 trillion marketplace, and with the pace of innovation accelerating, I feel confident that a flexible entrant like TeraExchange has more than a fighter's chance of thriving and providing a critical utility that's core to our story. Opportunities don't just happen; you have to create them. I'm enormously proud of the work, sensibilities, and courage displayed as I built this company, starting with just an idea and piloting the process through the earliest days to where we are now, excited about what the future looks like for us. "

THE WEISS-AUG GROUP
QUALITY. PRECISION. EXCELLENCE.

On April 19, 2018, Newark College of Engineering (NCE) at the New Jersey Institute of Technology Awarded Weiss-Aug Group founder Dieter Weissenrieder (class of '76) the Outstanding Alumnus Award at the twentieth annual NCE Salute to Engineering Excellence. The recognition might have been a long time coming, but it's a testament to Dieter that both he and his company are still thriving, innovating, and expanding more than four decades after he founded Weiss-Aug as a tool and die enterprise.

Now an industry leader for precision metal stamping, complex insert molding, and custom assembly, Dieter says the company constantly strives to expand their technology, capabilities, and performance "by joining forces with strategic organizations that reflect our culture, enhance our global footprint, augment our talent, and demonstrate a proven track record of servicing customers with the level of quality and professionalism that we've built Weiss-Aug's reputation on."

He believes that philosophy provides customers with unrivaled solutions for their custom component needs. It is also reflective of the attention to detail that he learned as a teenager in Germany and later as a tool and die maker journeyman for his uncle in the United States.

"I was born in Germany came to America in 1960 at age nineteen after a four-year apprenticeship in Germany as a tool and die maker," Dieter says. "The company I worked for wanted to send me to college—free of charge—and make an engineer out of me. Employers do that very frequently over there. My boss took me under his wing, and I'm very indebted to him because he helped me get a solid technical foundation under my feet."

But college would wait. Dieter's mother had two brothers living in the United States: one in Syracuse, New York, and the other one in New Jersey. Both were tool and die makers, as was their father, Dieter's grandfather.

"My uncles immigrated to America around the early to mid-1920s. And my uncle Leo eventually started his own little tool and die company here in Parsippany, New Jersey. My grandfather was also a tool and die maker. He had a small company with five or six employees that was totally destroyed during World War II. After the war he had nothing left but pretty much the clothes on his back, so his two sons wanted him to come to America."

Dieter's grandfather came to the United States in the early 1950s and stayed with his son Leo in New Jersey for about a year then returned to Germany. He came for another visit a few years later then again returned to Europe.

"My grandfather was a strong influence on why I came to America," Dieter says. "He said I should go even if for just a year to learn English and get familiar with what my uncle's company was doing over there. He paid for my ticket—which was one-way—and gave me a hundred bucks. I traveled by ocean liner, which was how most people traveled back then."

Dieter arrived in New York on February 9. "That date is always a big day for my family," he says. "In 2020 I celebrated my sixtieth anniversary of being here. That first day Uncle Leo picked me up and vouched for me. My second day here, I started working as a toolmaker in his little company that had about eight employees, and he paid me two dollars an hour, which was a lot of money in those days," he laughs. "My aunt and uncle had two daughters, and they took me in almost as a son. I had intended to come here

Dieter Weissenrieder

for two years, learn English, get to know America, and then return to Germany. But the opportunities in America were just too great, and I ended up staying."

Dieter lived with his uncle's family for the first couple of years he was in the United States. Not only did it provide a comfortable family environment, it helped him learn English. His two cousins only spoke English as did most of the people at work.

"The guy I worked next to helped me learn English, and he was a good teacher," Dieter says. "And as soon as I arrived, I started taking English courses at a local high school. Then a year later I had a girlfriend, and that helped tremendously. Learning the language was important. I knew I eventually wanted to go to college, so I had to make sure I had enough English under my belt to do that."

By 1965 the company had outgrown the facility in Parsippany and moved to a new, state-of-the-art plant in Montville. Dieter had moved up and was the shop's tool manager.

"When I arrived Uncle Leo was already up in age," Dieter says. "His daughters didn't want the business, which was good for me because when he started thinking about retirement around 1968, my uncle allowed me to buy a third of the company. And I ran the company as vice president of operations."

That same year Dieter married his wife Eleanor and started taking evening classes at NCE. "I realized that an industrial engineering degree was almost a must if my uncle's company continued growing, and I planned to be in a leadership position." Dieter also found that he enjoyed a familiarity with his classmates and instructors. "The evening student body consisted mostly of people who were in their late twenties and older, who had full-time jobs and were mostly married. I enjoyed it because professors were hands-on people who could relate to our kind of life."

In 1969 Uncle Leo bought a house in Florida and was ready to retire. The original plan was for him to sell his remaining shares to Dieter, who would then own and run the company.

"When I joined the company, we had eight employees. By 1969 we had fifty-five employees, a lot of great people. I really had fun growing the company."

But when Uncle Leo had the company appraised, it was valued at such a high amount that Dieter could not afford to buy him out within a reasonable amount of time. So in 1970 his aunt and uncle sold the business to Eaton Corporation, which was a large company based near Cleveland. Even though he got a third of the sale, Dieter admits he was initially extremely upset.

"But then a couple of years later I looked back and realized they had made the right decision. When you have a small family-run company like that, it holds all your assets other than your house. It was their nest egg. My uncle and aunt were concerned because in those days I had a short fuse. I was extremely competitive, and they were worried that if I ran the company while they still had a stake in it, I might lose their assets. They just wanted to be relaxing in Florida and not worry about it."

After Eaton bought out the company, Dieter felt like a bit of an afterthought to the new owner. "I was in my late twenties and an immigrant, so the lawyers looked at me like I was just some young ignorant kid. They told me that of course I would keep running the company, yet they wouldn't offer me an employment contract."

That should have been his first clue. Six months after the deal was struck, Eaton sent a manager from Cleveland to run the company. Dieter showed up to work one day to find he had a new boss.

"He was a good man," Dieter says diplomatically. "But he didn't know our industry. He didn't know our culture. And things went downhill from there." Dieter stayed with the company for a while but admits he was very unhappy. "In 1971 my wife finally said: *Rather than come home every night grouchy and mad, just get yourself another job, will you?*"

But after tasting the freedom of running a company on his own and working independently, he didn't want to work for someone else anymore. He needed to be on his own.

"So at the end of 1971, I decided to start my own manufacturing company and asked my chief engineer, Kurt Augustin, if he wanted to start the company with me. I had hired him in 1968. He came from Berlin and was four years older than me, and we became close friends. He said he wasn't happy with the new management either and agreed to start a new company with me, which we named Weiss-Aug."

They started the company in December 1971 as a side business. Ironically, they set up shop in his uncle's old building because he still owned the property. Dieter and Kurt worked weekends and evenings to get the business up and running.

"We were working long hours, but we were having fun. Then about six months into it, our boss got wind of what we were doing. One day in May I came into work on a Monday morning, and a couple of hours later, two executives showed up from Cleveland. It was a short conversation. They had a point that what I was doing was somewhat wrong, so I was fired."

When Kurt found out Dieter had been let go, he quit, and they put their undivided time and attention into Weiss-Aug. And over the next several weeks, Dieter says a dozen workers from the old company who were equally unhappy with the new management's culture and policies quit Eaton and joined Weiss-Aug.

"That's how we got a continuous supply of highly-qualified people," Dieter says. "Unfortunately five or six years later, Eaton gave up on the place and closed it down."

By that time Weiss-Aug was enjoying steady growth. Dieter says when compared to today, building a client base back in the 1970s was relatively easy if you were qualified and knew what you were doing.

Partial view of the stamping room

"Our industry isn't that big, so I was well-known from working at my uncle's company. People knew if they needed something done hat was impossible, there was this crazy German guy in New Jersey who could do it," he laughs. "So the first thing I did when we went on our own was to make a couple of phone calls and introduce myself now as a Weiss-Aug guy, not a Troy Tool Company guy. They were more loyal to me than they were to Eaton, so right away we got business coming in from various large former customers like RCA and Texas Instruments."

Dieter notes that back then, he dealt directly with the engineers rather than with purchasing, and a handshake was as good as a contract. The moment he shook on a deal, his company started working on the order. "I didn't have to worry that the other guy wouldn't make good. There's not that kind of trust anymore. Now everything is in writing first."

For the uninitiated, tool and die makers construct precision tools from steel, called dies, that are used to cut, shape, and form metal and other materials. Tool and diemakers also produce jigs that hold metal while it is bored, stamped, or drilled as well as gauges and other measuring devices. Dies are used to shape metal in stamping and forging operations.

"I would say about 15 percent of our business today is making dies, molds, and automation" Dieter says. "We have a design engineering department with about six engineers who design the dies and automation. We buy all our molds. When the die and automation design is complete, it goes to the tool room. We have a fairly large tool room with about twenty-five tool and die makers and mold makers."

When they started the company, both Dieter and Kurt built dies and ran manufacturing. But after a couple of years, Dieter slowly branched out of that and became more engineering- and sales-oriented, while Kurt stayed with the tooling end of it.

"I would say probably within three years or four years. I did not spend any time on the shop floor anymore," Dieter says. "I was more or less doing engineering sales and everything else that comes with it. And in the beginning I missed being on the floor. I'm the kind of guy who loves to work with my hands. But I also love to work with my brain. And in this business you need people that love to do both and are good in both areas."

In 1994 Kurt announced he was ready to hang up his tools. "He said: *It was your grand idea to start Weiss-Aug, I've been here for twenty happy years and now I'm ready to retire.* So I bought him out, and like my uncle, he moved to Florida."

Over the years Weiss-Aug continued to grow and evolve, adapting as technology changed and reshaped the industry, particularly in terms of specialization. When Dieter started, the design work was done by hand on a drawing board. Today's design engineers use computer-aided design (CAD) programs to develop blueprints for tooling, parts, and products. While some industries bemoan technology because it can take the place of workers, Dieter says the tremendous technological changes over the last forty years has helped the company grow and diversify.

"It is true that when new machinery was brought into the

marketplace, there were people who voiced the opinion that the machines were going to be the end of tool and die makers; they wouldn't be needed anymore," Dieter says. "Well, they were all wrong. They are still needed. It's just that they're not doing as much by hand. You still need them, you know, they're not as much involved in doing things by hand as we had to in the 1960s and '70s. Someone still has to run these complicated machines, someone with the right technical skillset. So more than ever you need workers who can use their brains rather than just working with their hands."

Despite the changing technology, Dieter says the business itself has not changed. "If I showed a customer an item we made forty years ago alongside the same order that was made yesterday, they wouldn't be able to tell them apart because the complexity, the type of metal—everything is still the same except it goes into a different end product today. Yes, the machinery is more advanced, it's computer-controlled, but the tool and die maker is still very much needed."

Over Weiss-Aug's company lifetime, it's gone through many chapters. In the first ten years, it went from part-time endeavor to entrepreneurial start-up to successful fast-growth business, each level marked by evolving products and services. Since then acquisition has been an integral part of Dieter's growth strategy, evolving the Weiss-Aug company into the Weiss-Aug Group.

"Until 1980 we were strictly a stamping company, making stamped components for many industries including electronics, automotive, and medical," Dieter says. "Then in 1980 we had an opportunity to buy a small company that was in the molding business. That enabled us to branch out into mold-making and produce very precise and complicated plastic parts."

Dieter expanded and moved the company to East Hanover, the site where Dieter is based. "We have actually two manufacturing plants that are connected to each other, covering one hundred thousand square feet. One is a molding plant, and the other one is a stamping plant."

As they got more heavily into medical instruments, Weiss-Aug purchased their third plant less than ten miles away from East Hanover in 2017 that is dedicated solely to medical instruments. The company also opened up a plant in Apodaca, Mexico—near Monterey—that right now is strictly for medical products, and the facility also has both stamping and molding capability, but Dieter notes that plant is still in its infancy, but rapidly expanding.

At the end of 2019, Weiss-Aug agreed to purchase the remaining third of a stamping plant in Chicago that Dieter had bought a two-thirds majority interest in four years earlier. The sale was finalized in January of 2020. Weiss-Aug also owns a plant near Pittsburgh that is strictly for building tools, dies, and jigs. And in early 2020 the company finalized establishing a research and development laboratory in Colorado, where in-house scientists are developing products and processes for the medical industry.

While all founders should have an exit strategy, the bigger the company, the more crucial that strategy becomes because it impacts so many individuals. Today's business model for many entrepreneurs is to build a company fast, sell it for a profit, then look to start another company. Wash, rinse, repeat. But businesses that start as family enterprises tend to have different priorities.

Unlike Uncle Leo's daughters who had no interest in carrying on the tool

Partial view of the medical molding department

and die legacy, Dieter expects to pass down Weiss-Aug to his children. "Although I still feel young up in my head, I am getting up in age. Luckily I have a daughter and a son. Both have been working in the business during the summers since they were in high school because they enjoyed the business and loved being here."

Now adults, Dieter says both of his children are heavily involved in the company, and he has zero plans to sell the company. More than even the bad taste of Eaton still lingering all these decades later, experience tells him it's not a winning move for the company.

"Forget investment sales. I've seen too many competitors sell to investment companies, then within about five years those companies that sold are all dead. I feel too close to my employees to do that to them. I have so many managers who have been with me for thirty or more years. One of my original employees is retiring next week after forty-two years, so we're throwing them a big party. These people are more than employees. They are friends; they are family. I tell you now unless it were a strategic sale, and there are not too many of those,"

Dieter says he had a heart-to-heart with his children a few years ago while on a ski trip. He gave them a choice: *Let's talk business. Do you want me to keep the company, or do you want me to sell it?*

"They both said: *Dad, of course we want the business.* And I was the happiest guy. So my daughter has been groomed to run the company when I retire. She is a great business lady. My son is more drawn to the technical side. My daughters' husband is also in the company and was just promoted to sales manager. And I have a six-year-old grandson who is already walking through the plant right now, always wanting to watch the big machines. I tell you; he's going to be ready to be a part of Weiss-Aug someday too. So we're going to keep the company growing."

Having been in the industry on two continents for more than half a century, Dieter has acquired a treasure trove of hands-on experience, strategic knowledge, and hard-earned lessons learned. One of the most important points he has passed on to his kids is that the biggest downside to any business in their industry is becoming too financially oriented or feeling entitled to the keys of the company kingdom without having put in any sweat equity.

At least in the United States, expectations of nepotistic entitlement are probably why so few family-run companies survive past the second generation. Dieter's perspective is no doubt colored by his immigrant experience and having started at the bottom of his uncle's company —nothing came easily, so each achievement was all the sweeter. And he wants his children and grandchildren to experience that kind of professional joy and satisfaction.

"What I told my children, and what I will tell my grandson, is you need to know the business from the ground up," Dieter says. "You have to know what's happening on the shop floor. I tell you; I see too many families make the same mistake where they say: *I had it rough. I had a tough. I want to have my kids have it simpler, easier. I don't want them to go through a struggle.* I think that's baloney."

Dieter fervently believes there is no better education and character-building than starting at the bottom rung and working your way up. "Don't pull a college graduate in here who says: *Well, I've got these big degrees on the wall, so I know how to run a company.* You do not truly know how to run a company unless you start from the bottom on up."

It was a philosophy his children learned first-hand. Dieter told them both that they could not work at Weiss-Aug until they had gone elsewhere and worked for some other company for at least three years.

"I said: *You want to work here? Okay, go get your butt kicked in, and then if you still want to come back here, you can come back,*" Dieter says.

"So both worked for three years somewhere else, and then they had a choice: either stay where they were, making a good living, or come back and start from the ground up here. Both decided to come back. I would do the same thing with my grandchildren. You cannot pass something on a plate and say: *Okay, here; just take it and run with it.* No, they have to earn it."

His advice to up-and-coming engineers interested in the tool and die industry follows along the same line. "Part of an engineer's education must be hands-on. You need practical experience in the industry before graduating, so I strongly recommend students use their summer vacations to work as an intern. Four years of just academics are simply not enough. Like anything else, if you put your time to good use by learning all you can from the bottom up, you are setting yourself up for success regardless of whether you want to be the best employee somewhere or build a company like I did with Weiss-Aug."

L-R: Mr. Jeff Cole, *vice president of operations*; Mr. Dieter Weissenrieder, *president*; Mrs. Elisabeth Weissenrieder-Bennis, *executive vice president*; and Mr. Mark Weissenrieder, *IT/automation manager*.

WITTMAN GROUP

In the early morning hours of September 2, 1666, a fire broke out in the house of King Charles II's baker on Pudding Lane near London Bridge. Pushed by a strong wind, the flames quickly spread to nearby warehouses filled with combustibles, creating an unstoppable inferno. By the time the Great Fire of London was finally extinguished four days later, more than 80 percent of London was reduced to ash. More than thirteen homes, eighty-seven churches, and most of the city's municipal buildings were destroyed. The financial loss was equally catastrophic because at the time insurance didn't exist. That would soon change.

As a direct result of the fire, several new laws were passed to mitigate future fire losses, including a mandate for the incorporation of an organization to indemnify losses due to fire, which led to a well-known physician cum economist named Nicholas Barbon to found the first insurance company, called the Fire Office. His motives were hardly altruistic. Much of his wealth was invested in properties, and he didn't want his assets to go up in smoke. He assembled teams whose sole job was to put out fires in the buildings the company insured. Other companies soon followed.

There were inherent issues with having dueling private firefighting forces, so London and other cities eventually established municipal fire departments. By then the need for insurance beyond fire was firmly established, and over the centuries the industry grew and expanded. While society may have evolved, the basic tenet of insurance remained: a promise to reimburse policyholders for losses in exchange for regular payments called premiums.

Today insurance is considered so essential that it is legally required in certain instances, such as when driving a car. But even when not mandated, most people and businesses can't afford *not* to have insurance, so there's an inherent resentment in having to pay for something you may never use or need. More than that is the perception by many consumers that insurance companies go out of their way to make it difficult for policyholders to collect on legitimate claims, and surveys over the last decade have shown that the majority of people simply don't trust insurance companies to do right by them.

The Wittman Group, which specializes in personal and commercial insurance and retirement consulting for small business owners, has set out to change that narrative. Founder Peter Wittman says his company's mission is to "build lasting client relationships based on trust that is earned through wise counsel, positive results, clear and candid communication, and service that exceeds expectations. We are transparent in our dealings and provide personalized advice—often without payment—to help clients make better-informed decisions, which underscores our commitment to putting the best interests of the client first."

Pop culture often depicts salesmen as slick wheeler-dealers more concerned with their close rate than being of service to the client. But for Peter a personal approach to clients is second nature. The son of missionaries, he spent his teen years in Australia before returning to the United States, where he planned to get a degree in mechanical engineering at the University of Delaware.

"I needed a way to pay for school," Peter says. "A guy from Southwestern came on campus and said you could make $5,000 that summer selling books door-to-door. This was back before the Internet,

Peter Wittman

when students had to go to a library and look for resources when they had a research paper to write."

Southwestern Company started by selling Bibles door-to-door just after the Civil War, then over the years it moved more toward reference and educational books covering academic subjects such as history and math, covering middle school grades to college level. Today Southwestern also sells software, still using the same door-to-door business model.

"Every summer they would take about four thousand college kids, bring them to Nashville, and put them through seventy hours of boot camp sales training," Peter says. "Then they'd send those who survived the camp to a different part of the country where they didn't know anybody and have them sell books door-to-door, earning a 40 percent commission."

Peter spent each summer during his undergraduate years at college selling books. His first city was Port Huron, Michigan. With each knock on a new door, he honed his people and entrepreneurial skills. "Selling books door-to-door, you essentially ran your own business," he says. "You were responsible for the sales, for your expenses, and for your inventory. on your books."

He worked six days a week, logging about eighty hours. He estimated he called on three thousand people. "It was hard work, the school of hard knocks. But at the end of my first summer in 1989, I made $8,900 selling books for ten weeks' work. Back then that was a lot of money. I was able to write a check for my entire year's tuition before I came back from Michigan."

Beyond having missionary parents and spending time overseas,

Peter says another significant influence on who he is today was growing up with a congenital anomaly. "I was the sixth of six kids. I was a high-risk pregnancy; my mom had me when she was forty. I was born with my left hand fused. The bones were there, just not in the right places. So when I was two, they cut it open in the middle. My hand looked like Pac-Man if you looked at it in the shadows."

As a kid, especially during middle school, Peter endured the stares and comments. But as a collegiate door-to-door salesman, he'd use his hand and self-deprecating humor to disarm people.

"When I sold books, I'd tell people: *The best part about my books is they don't cost an arm and a leg, just a couple of fingers.* And then I would show them my hand. It was a great icebreaker."

Beginning with his third summer, Southwestern promoted Peter to a field manager, put him in charge of a team of ten sellers, and sent him to Lancaster, California, an hour north of Los Angeles. He spent his fourth year in Castle Rock, Colorado, which was between Denver and Colorado Springs, in charge of twenty-five sellers.

Southwestern promoted Peter to assistant sales manager, where he recruited and trained a forty-person organization, which generated $150,000 of business in three months. But the wear and tear of the position gave him pause.

"The travel was brutal. I was leaving out on Sunday night and coming home Saturday afternoon. I didn't know if I really wanted that life."

In 1989 Southwestern established Family Heritage Life Insurance Company of America as a supplemental insurance company. Peter's sales manager for three of his book-selling summers was now at Family Heritage and offered him a job.

"He said: *Look, you won't have to travel, and you can learn insurance.* And I'm thinking, *I don't want to learn insurance,*" Peter says with a laugh. "But I took the job."

Over the next six years, first at Family Heritage then General Insurance Underwriters, he learned the industry, advancing from a sales rep to a trainer to a district manager. When Peter left General in 2000, they sent a letter reminding him he had signed a non-compete agreement.

"I couldn't work at another company selling insurance for two years," he says. "They could have come after me, so I needed to do something in-between. I went back to Southwestern and asked where I could go. They offered me a job headhunting and said I could pick whatever industry I wanted. So I headhunted people mostly for insurance companies."

When his non-compete ran out, Peter worked with a company called American Medical Security, recruiting, and training independent agents and brokers. "They eventually got bought out by PacifiCare, so that sucked," he says with a laugh. "But then Gale Smith and Company basically hired me on the spot."

For the entrepreneurial-minded, there an advantage in working for many companies: not only do you learn things you would want to do if you were in charge, you also learned what you don't want to do.

"Rather than finding out what was right for the client, too often it was all about selling more insurance," Peter says. "Let's just sell them some more insurance, another product. The last company I worked for was selling plans that the IRS basically made illegal, by removing their tax deductibility. But even after the government said to stop selling those, the company kept selling them anyway. The agency ended up with a large errors and omissions claim against it."

Peter admits that the writing was on the wall, and he should have moved on. "As my wife would say: *You always wait until someone kicks you out before you go.* I try to hang on. I'm just persistent that way, in hopes that it works out. The eternal optimist who believes it will get better. Gale Smith decided to sell the company and put it on the market. To make their books look good, they basically got rid of all the younger producers, so it would make their profit margin look that much better without the expense of having to pay somebody. I was fourth on the list, and they had already canned the three guys before me."

But Peter says he rocked the boat because they had neglected to have him sign a non-compete. It somehow had slipped through the cracks.

"So after they canned me, they called me back and said; *You need to come in and sign this non-compete.* I said: *In exchange for what?* They go: *What do you mean?* I go: *In exchange for what? You want me to sign a non-compete after the fact. I'm going to need some compensation for that.* They said they were going to get an attorney. I told them to go ahead; they knew where to find me."

In the end Peter's attorney sent a letter, and the non-compete issue went away at least from a legal standpoint. He started interviewing with several other agencies before having an epiphany.

"I remember thinking: *This is getting out of the frying pan and into the fire* because the way they structured those agencies were the same way. In the 2000s everybody wanted to be like Marsh, a big national super-broker. They wanted to have salespeople go and sell insurance then pass it to a service person. And the service person would then manage that block of business, and the salesperson would never be seen again. He would move onto the next sale. That's the way the industry was heading and where it is today. Turn the TV on and you've got Flo, you've got a duck, a gecko. We've got an emu selling car insurance. And Pinocchio. But I didn't grow up that way. I grew up with: if you're selling it, you need to service it. People are buying your knowledge base; they're not just buying a product off the shelf."

Still the best ice breaker.

Peter says we're becoming conditioned to shopping for insurance online. "You go to a site and it says: *Only buy what you need.* It should be saying: *Only buy what you want to pay for* because most of the time people don't know what they need. I talk to people, and they don't understand what split limits means. They don't understand what uninsured motorist is. But if I tell them the story of Barbara, where an underinsured nineteen-year-old came across the middle of the highway and hit her head-on, so Barbara and her daughter were in intensive care for more than forty-five days. Because they had uninsured motorist coverage, her insurance paid for all their medical bills and replacing the car everything because the teenager had minimum limits on his car, which was $15,000 at that time, which didn't go very far. When people hear that, it becomes real. They understand what uninsured and underinsured motorist means in real-world terms. But most people just go online and look for the cheapest price."

When he started his own insurance agency, Peter wanted to specialize in insurance for small businesses, customizing solutions to protect entrepreneurs against the pitfalls that could threaten their businesses. "There are inherent problems that small businesses have, which is one reason why most small businesses don't make it to ten years."

Peter says Michael Gerber's 1985 book *The E-Myth: Why Most Businesses Don't Work and What to Do About It* had a profound impact on his thinking and awareness. The E-myth—entrepreneurial myth—is the (mistaken) belief that most businesses are started by people with tangible business skills, when in fact most are started by technicians who know nothing about running a business. Hence most fail. Or put another way, it's a mistake to think that individuals who understand the technical work of a business can automatically successfully run a business that does that technical work.

"Gerber broke down a business into three stages—infancy, adolescence, and maturity," Peter explains. "At each stage there are pitfalls for an entrepreneur. During infancy when the owner does everything, if something happens like a fall or car accident that leaves you laid up even for just a little while, it can be insurmountable, so you need to protect yourself against that. During adolescence is when you realize you can't do everything and start hiring employees and delegating responsibility. Now you need workers' comp insurance; otherwise, the owner is responsible for all medical bills is an employee is hurt on the job. For a mature business, taxes or a liability issue can take you out if you're not careful. So depending on where your company is, you need insurance designed for your specific situation. But you'd be amazed at how many entrepreneurs tell me: *I don't need insurance.*"

Peter says he learned about the importance of workers' comp when a pastor at a Church fell down the church basement stairs while carrying a heavy box. He broke both legs and a bunch of ribs. On top of that he laid at the bottom of the steps for nearly twelve hours before someone found him. That workers' comp claim for the ensuing medical bills was more than a million dollars.

"The church had not spent the money on workers' comp because they weren't required to by Tennessee law because they only had two employees: the pastor and church secretary. So they were responsible for all that cost. Those are the *gotchas* that can wreck your company."

Another reason small businesses need an expert like Peter instead of a do-it-yourself website is that insurance laws have gotten more complicated over the years, particularly since Congress passed the Health

Insurance Portability and Accountability Act (HIPAA) in 1996, which restricted the dissemination of healthcare information.

"When I sold my first group benefit plan prior to HIPAA, there were eleven federal laws related to health insurance. Now you have thirty-six hundred pages of the Patient Protection and Affordable Care Act. Even the Cliff Notes version was a hundred pages," he jokes.

Peter says he started the Wittman Group with a business partner, who he credits with teaching him a lot about retirement plans. "That was his specialty. My expertise was largely in group benefits, so I would create solutions for small business owners. That first year we put a lot of business on the books. We took the agency from zero to $290,000 in revenue. Then I got blackballed by my former employer—the one who didn't get a non-compete. I learned that he was calling carriers and telling them: *If you give him a contract, we'll move our business from you.*"

Which, of course, at the very least is not ethical. But for Peter it was another lesson learned.

"I would tell people if you're going to start an insurance agency from scratch, know that it's really difficult to get contracts, no matter who you are because all of them want volume right away. I finally found one company to give me a contract, and then I found the Strategic Independent Agents Alliance, which was a cluster group. In exchange for a percentage of whatever commission I made, they would give me access to about fifty different companies. It was a good trade-off, and that's what we did to get contracts."

From that point on the company got traction. By the end of May 2008, he and his partner had split. In retrospect his experience is a cautionary tale for any entrepreneur thinking of having a partnership.

"We had worked together well before then, but after we signed on the dotted line, issues came up. I didn't understand we needed to have things in writing about how our partnership should go. I learned the huge lesson that you'd better have written ground rules for your partnership before you sign the paperwork."

Having to adjust to a new normal, Peter says the company expanded its reach into the music industry. "One of my employees had strong ties to some managers, who basically control all the financials, including insurance and retirement planning. But what we didn't have was the insurance contracts to write that business. So we found a group out of London that had worked with Mick Jagger and a host of other musicians and entertainers, which had the pen to write the insurance. They later approached me about taking them on as a group and splitting my house in half so that half of my agency would be music- and entertainment-related, and the other half would be general lines, which I had experience in."

Peter put his top employee in charge of working through the details with the London group while he was working through the end of the partnership. Then came Friday, November 14, 2008.

"I went to the office, and nobody showed up for work. At 11:00 the guy I had put in charge of London came in and announced he and my other two employees were all moving over to the group in London. *He decided it's not worth it for him to partner with you but to just take us as employees and pay us and open up a shop down the street. And by the way, we're taking all our business with us. But don't worry, Pete. You're going to be fine.*"

Gut punch number two. Peter admits he needed a moment—or two—to regroup.

"When my partner left me holding the bag on $350,000 of debt, I had thought: *I'm going to be okay. These guys were going to keep producing, and it's going to be fine.* Now that was gone. My last employee, my assistant, got another job because he was afraid we weren't going to be around much longer. I was scared we weren't going to be around too. When growing up, my mom would often say: *There's too much month at the end of the money*. And there were several times throughout running this business when there was too much month. Everybody got paid before me. I didn't take a paycheck until 2010. I lived off my savings, and we went through everything in that process. But I believed in what we were doing to get to where we're at. I was persistent. And after losing my staff, I learned every job of the agency very quickly. And about six months later I managed to hire a really good person who helped me through a lot of that."

Peter had thought that his staff was generating most of the Wittman Group's business. Once he did an audit, he discovered he was the prime contract driver.

"So we survived. Even though it was a gut punch, we worked our butts off and crawled out of that and moved forward. As an entrepreneur, you must make sure you're constantly adapting to what's going on, which means you can't put all of your eggs in one method of doing business. You have to be willing to adapt and anticipate changing markets."

And to changing technology. Digital technology has touched every industry in some fashions, and for agents like Peter, it's created new challenges.

"Liberty Mutual is one of the companies that we sell for. But they're on TV advertising LiMu Emu. *Go online at libertymutual.com, and get yourself a quote.* Progressive is another company that we represent, but you can get it direct online too. So technology is taking the agent out of the mix because of the commoditization of the product. And there's always going to be a segment that's going to go for the easiest and the cheapest."

Between online technology and the Affordable Care Act, insurance agencies like Wittman Group needed to evolve. "When you first get into business, you're just hungry for a deal and will write up any contract. Then

I decided I was just going to target small businesses. Then the Affordable Care Act came in, and I was back to: *Hey, we'll write up anybody*. Now I've come back full circle. The people I best serve are entrepreneurs and their families. They're running a business, they've got a home, and they've got a couple of cars. Maybe their kids are starting to drive. If you want to boil it down, our target is middle-class millionaires or future middle-class millionaires, people who will be when they retire because they're putting money away. Those are the clients that fit with the best rates offered by the companies we have contracts with. That's how we define our target market. And in truth, that may change again. The lesson learned from the Affordable Care Act is you have to be willing to change and adapt accordingly. And with the way things change, you need to reassess about every five years otherwise you're going to be left behind."

Peter admits going online for insurance is faster, but you're exchanging speed for expertise and personalized consulting. "In terms of adapting, you're finding out what the client's needs are and filling those needs. For example, we're going through a phase in our society where people are highly litigious. Most small businesses, especially start-ups, don't realize that if you're a small retail business in Tennessee still swiping cards instead of using a chip reader, if that customer's identity gets compromised, you're responsible for seven times the amount of the breach. And for a small business owner, that's a big number, so if you don't have insurance to cover, that you are in trouble."

Even if there was a breach with no money taken, the business owner would still have to send out a letter saying there was a breach and pay for a year's worth of credit monitoring for each customer. "That's going to cost you about $400 for each piece of data entry you have in your system. So if you have one thousand people in your system, that's $400,000. Most small businesses don't have a big enough cash reserve to write a check that big.

That's just one of the many hiccups that could take out a small business. Now, if you're buying your insurance over the Internet, do they tell you all that?"

So Peter says his latest adaptation is that he's no longer an insurance agent. He's a consultant who helps small business owners learn about the pitfalls that could wreck their business.

"I'm here to help so that if any pitfall arises, you are not wrecked. I also can provide other valuable information along the way as well, such as when you are or are not liable to settle a claim. But the bottom line is, while we've adapted—I'm no longer the insurance guy or the retirement guy or the benefits guy, now I'm the consultant guy—I really haven't changed Wittman Group's core values, which have always been: *We're here to help small businesses.*"

Peter acknowledges having an insurance consultant is not for everyone. He knows many small businesses prefer a DIY, *Just give me the information, I'll go handle it myself* approach, even when it's not efficient.

"As Michael Gerber says in *E-Myth*, that is very typical of small business owners. And I know that from my own experience. I've had to learn some valuable lessons, such as you can't walk through business without systems in place, and you have to always be willing to adapt."

Perhaps at the heart of his current business philosophy is the effort to be uncommon. "We don't want to do what the other guys are doing," Peter says. "I've learned that if everybody's going in the same direction, I should go in a different direction. My wife says I'm just a rebel."

As a kid in Australia, Peter worked on a sheep farm, and he recalls how the animals really would all follow one another. Even if there was no particular reason why, they would just go with the crowd.

"I don't want to be sheep. I want to be the uncommon person that's going the other way. And that's what we try to do at Wittman Group. More than just consulting, I want to be educational. I want to teach my clients what they should be thinking about. And that's been the impetus for the adaptation. Clients have needs. Clients have wants. And we give them customized solutions. There's no off-the-rack service here."

About Creative Classics Inc.

Creative Classics Inc. was born thirty years ago in Canada with a mandate to write, publish, and market entertaining, insightful, and informative high-end books.

The company's first book, *The Wizards: Millionaire Magicians of the Vancouver Stock Market*, was launched in spring 1988. Within six months, it hit the Canadian Bestseller List.

Over the next twenty-five years, the Creative Classics team wrote and published another twenty-two books including: *Gold Rush*: companies searching for the world's most precious metal; *Above and Beyond the Glass Ceiling*: women who have shattered barriers in the business world; *The Great, Green Gold Rush*: the pioneers, former outlaws, and innovators forging the legal cannabis industry, and *Made in the USA*: entrepreneurs bullish on keeping the tradition of manufacturing home-grown American products alive and well.

With *The American Entrepreneur*, Creative Classics again showcases some of today's most innovative entrepreneurs who are poised to lead their industries into the rapidly changing business world of tomorrow.